A World of Turtles

A WORLD OF TURTLES

A Literary Celebration

Edited by Gregory McNamee
and Luis Alberto Urrea

JOHNSON BOOKS
Boulder

Published in the United States by Johnson Books, a division of Johnson Publishing Company, 1880 South 57th Court, Boulder, Colorado 80301.

9   8   7   6   5   4   3   2   1

Cover design: Debra B. Topping
Cover artwork © 1996 by Shauna L. Decker

Library of Congress Cataloging-in-Publication Data
    A world of turtles: a literary celebration / edited by Gregory McNamee and Luis Alberto Urrea.
        p.   cm.
    Includes bibliographical references.
    ISBN 1-55566-190-4 (pbk.: alk. paper)
    1. Turtles—Anecdotes.   2. Turtles—Folklore.   3. Turtles.
I. McNamee, Gregory.   II. Urrea, Luis Alberto.
QL795.T8W67   1997
597.92—dc21   97-25623
                                                                                        CIP

Printed in the United States by
Johnson Printing
1880 South 57th Court
Boulder, Colorado 80301

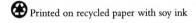 Printed on recycled paper with soy ink

CONTENTS

INTRODUCTION

A few weeks ago, just after the mild Sonoran Desert winter had given way to the first heat of spring, I went out to a small arroyo draining the northeastern flank of Baboquívari Peak, the sacred mountain of the Tohono O'odham people. It is a place to which I often repair for one reason or another: to watch merlins and tanagers, to walk idly, to sit under a streamside mesquite tree and think. This time, however, I came on a mere hunch that on that particular day, at this particular little patch of rock and sand, I might happen on a desert tortoise or two and secure some kind of chelonian blessing for the book you are now reading. I was not disappointed. Within a few minutes an old dirt-encrusted *Xerobates agassizii* poked its head from around a clump of tallgrass, looked myopically in my general direction but ignored my call of greeting, and lumbered off into the rocks.

We take our blessings where we can, and the sight of that single *Xerobates*, that wizened bodhisattva of the arroyos, was enough for me that day, at the cusp of turtle season. The Tohono O'odham evidently feel the same way; traditionally, the sight of a single desert tortoise was a good omen, and anyone who impeded such a creature's progress invited disaster and illness. Come the hotter months, there will likely be more *Xerobates* in that place, a phalanx bearing the possibilities of good fortune, and a wonderful sight to behold. An all-too-rare *Kinosternon sonoriense*, the largest mud turtle in the United States, may even show up.

But of such things I must write in the conditional, for the numbers of turtles are declining here in the Sonoran Desert: harvested for meat and oil, run over by crosscountry motorcycles, condemned to death by the loss of habitat and breeding ground. Elsewhere in the country the situation is much the same; as Mike Bryan writes in *Uneasy Rider* (Knopf, 1997), his genial tour of the interstates, one fellow working a few small east Texas lakes figures to pull out 200,000 red-eared, snapper, box, and soft-shelled turtles each year to sell to the trade. Contrary to this man's business plan, turtles are not an endlessly renewable resource—but they are, luckily for him and unluckily for them, easy to catch.

The pattern holds elsewhere in the world. In Costa Rica, hundreds and thousands of olive ridley eggs disappear from nesting grounds each year, to be sold and consumed for their reputed aphrodisiac properties. The plowshare tortoise of Madagascar, now a commodity traded in the black market for $20,000 a head, may disappear from the wild in our lifetime, to live only in a few zoos and private collections. The world's population of sea turtles, by United Nations estimates, has been cut in half in the last twenty years. In deserts, woodlands, mountains, and plains, like statistics are being racked up.[*]

Could it be that turtles, those ancient reminders of the Age of Reptiles—they first appeared in the Triassic, about 200 million years ago—are going the way of so many other species in this chewed-up and spat-out time? The available evidence suggests that, sadly, this may be so. I can only hope not; I want to be able to endorse in my own

---

[*] *Turtle* is the epicene term for turtles, tortoises, and terrapins. Turtles are both aquatic and terrestrial; tortoises are terrestrial only; and terrapins are confined to salt-water coastal areas. Land turtles are almost always herbivorous and defensive, sea turtles almost always carnivorous and aggressive.

time the ancient Chinese belief that the universe rests on the backs of turtles, constant symbols of strength, patience, endurance, and long life. (Never mind another ancient Chinese belief: namely, that turtles are only female, and that they reproduce by mating with snakes and dragons.)

This book, which gathers literary sightings of turtles over many times and many cultures, is a testimonial to that hope: a small effort to raise, if you'll forgive the phrase, turtle consciousness. Those of us who live in the United States have several opportunities to turn that consciousness into action, for of the 240-odd species of turtles worldwide, 49 of them are found in this country; of the world's seven species of true sea turtles, six live in North American waters; four tortoise species are unique to the United States. Each demands our respect. Each merits our protection, and in this we have much work to do, cataloging their number, studying their habits and life histories, determining ways that our world might be made safe for the ancient reptiles. As a very small contribution to this effort, I am donating royalties from this book to a number of turtle-conservation organizations, whose collective work has lately been improving the fortunes of several species.

For their help and advice in making this book, I thank Kim Long, Steve Topping, Liliana Slomkowska, and Robert McCord. I also thank Luis Alberto Urrea, who conceived the idea for an anthology on turtles and helped edit a portion of this collection.

Gregory McNamee

Testudo the Tortoise is so called because his shell is like a pot (*testa*) that covers him. There are these kinds: land tortoises, sea tortoises, mud tortoises that live in filthy marshes, and a fourth kind, found in rivers, that delights in fresh water. I have heard this incredible fact told: that ships sail more slowly if on board they carry the right foot of a tortoise.

—*Medieval Latin bestiary*

What are they saying
of the planets and the turtles?

—*Kenneth Patchen*

TURTLE ISLAND
Abenaki myth

Many Native American cultures call the North American continent Turtle Island, a name that owes its origins to a complex of continent-wide myths about Turtle, who bears the earth on its back. This is one such myth.

Once a woman fell from her home way up in the sky. As she fell, she grabbed hold of a tree and pulled loose a handful of seeds. She fell far, far down, until she finally landed in a great ocean.

The birds and animals who lived in the ocean called a council to discuss what they would do with her. After a while, they decided to make the earth so that she would have someplace to live.

One by one, the birds and animals swam to the ocean floor and tried to bring up mud. All of them failed, except Muskrat, who is an exceptionally strong swimmer.

"Where will we put this mud?" the animals asked each other.

Turtle replied, "Put it on my back."

And Muskrat kept swimming down to the ocean floor, bringing up mud, while the animals packed the earth on Turtle's back. Turtle grew larger and larger, until at last the woman had a place to live. She climbed up on Turtle's back and planted the seeds she had gathered, and that is how the land on which we live was made.

THE CREATION
Maidu folktale

The famed anthropologist A. E. Kroeber recorded this myth of the Maidu, a Native people of central California, in the early 1900s.

In the beginning there was no light, and everywhere there was water.

From the north a raft came, carrying Turtle. A feather rope fell down from the sky. Earth Starter came down the rope, tied it to the raft, and boarded it. He wore a mask, but through it his face shone like the very sun. Earth Starter sat there quietly, looking at Turtle.

"Where did you come from?" Turtle asked.

"From way up there," said Earth Starter, pointing at the sky.

"I would like it if you would make me some dry land to stand on now and then," said Turtle. "Will you be putting people on the earth?"

"Yes, I will," Earth Starter replied.

"When will you do that?"

"Sometime. If you want me to make you some dry land, though, you will have to get me some earth."

Turtle got ready to dive under the water to find some earth. Earth Starter tied a rock around Turtle's wrist and tied the feather rope to Turtle's leg.

"If the rope is not long enough, I'll give it a single tug," Turtle said. "If it is long enough, I'll get some earth and then tug on the rope twice, and then you can pull me up."

Then he dove over the side. But he stayed down there under the water for six years. When he came up, he was covered with mud. He had only a little bit of earth, stuck under his claws. Earth Starter scraped this earth from Turtle's claws and rolled it in his hands. The little ball grew and grew until it was as big as the world.

"Good," said Turtle. "Now can you make some light?"

So Earth Starter called his sister, the Sun, from the east, and his brother, the Moon, from the west. And so the earth and its light were created.

KANA RESCUES HINA
Hawai'ian myth

The Hawai'ian demigod Kana is a "stretching kupua," a shape-shifting divinity who manifests himself in various landforms, as this telegraphic myth relates.

The firstborn of Hakalanileo and Hina is born, looking like a rope. His grandmother Uli raises him in the uplands of Pi'ihonua, beyond Hilo, in a grass house called Halau-ololo.

As the child grows, the house has to grow, too, from the mountains to sea, in order to contain him. For he is a stretching kupua, and nothing can hold him.

Chief Kapepe'ekauila sails over to the island of Moku-ola, using the hill Haupu as his canoe. Hina climbs up that hill to take a look around, and Kapepe'ekauila carries her off to become his wife.

Hakalanileo appeals for help to his son Niheu, who sends him to Kana. But Hakalanileo flees at the sight of Kana's fiery eyes. Kana organizes a war party, but two times he sinks the canoes, for he has grown so large. Finally Uli finds the magical canoe Kaumaielieli in the uplands of Paliuli, and the war party sails.

In vain the prophet Moi warns Kapepe'ekauila of defeat. Kapepe'ekauila orders his warriors to climb the hill and defend it from attack. The messenger birds Kolea, Plover, and Ulili, Snipe, go off to reconnoiter, while Moi sends the monster turtle Keauleinakahi to destroy the canoe.

A great battle ensues. Kana's body is huge now, and he stretches it out like a spider web to his grandmother's door so that she can give him counsel. Uli tells him that the hill Haupu is really a giant turtle named Kahonunuimaeleka, who can stretch its flippers around the world. Kana goes off to do battle with the giant turtle. He crushes Kahonunuimaeleka's back, tossing bits of bloody shell into the ocean all around him, and returns Hina to her husband.

From the pieces of the hill Haupu come the turtles that today swim in the waters of Hawai'i.

Another Hawai'ian myth ascribes shapeshifting powers to turtles themselves. In this, an old couple takes in a turtle named Kawaimalino. Some children of the village accidentally poke Kawaimalino's eye out with a sharpened stick. That night, a ghostly woman missing one eye visits the couple in their dreams and implores them to return the turtle to its home in the Wailuku River. They do so, and the horrifying visitation ends.

REFLECTIONS ON
A TORTOISE

Gilbert White

Do turtles have an elephant's memory? Evidently so, according to Gilbert White, who observed them closely and recorded his findings in The Natural History of Selborne *(1789). A good churchman, White also chided the tortoise for its laziness while remarking with wonder on the one thing that gets a chelonian moving.*

While I was at Sussex last autumn my residence was at the village near Lewes, from whence I formerly had the pleasure of writing to you. On the first of November I remarked that an old tortoise ... began first to dig the ground, in order to form its hypernaculum, which it had fixed on just beside a great tuft of hepaticas. It scrapes out the ground with its fore-feet, and throws it up over its back with its hind; but the motion of its legs is ridiculously slow, little exceeding the hour-hand of a clock; and suitable to the composure of an animal said to be a whole month in performing one feat of copulation. Nothing can be more assiduous than this creature night and day in scooping the earth, and forcing its great body into the cavity; but as the noons of that season proved unusually warm and sunny, it was continually interrupted, and called forth by the heat in the middle of the day: and though I continued there till the thirteenth of November, yet the work remained unfinished. Harsher weather, and frosty mornings, would have quickened its operations. No part of its behaviour ever struck me more than the extreme timidity it always expresses with regard to rain; for though it has a shell that would secure it against the wheel of a loaded cart, yet does it discover as much solicitude about rain as a lady dressed in all her best attire, shuffling away on the first sprinklings, and running its head up in a corner. If attended to it becomes an excellent weather-glass: for as sure as it walks elate, and as it were on tiptoe, feeding with great earnestness in a morning, so sure will it rain before night. It is totally a diurnal animal, and never pretends to stir after it becomes dark. The tortoise, like other reptiles, has an arbitrary stomach as well as lungs; and can refrain from eating as well as breathing for a great part of the year. When first awakened it eats nothing; nor again in the autumn before it retires: through the height of the summer it feeds voraciously, devouring all the food that comes in its way. I was much taken with its sagacity in discerning those that do it kind offices; for as soon as the good old lady comes in sight who has waited on it for more than thirty years, it hobbles towards its benefactress with awkward alacrity; but remains inattentive to strangers. Thus not only "the ox knoweth its owner, and the ass his master's crib."

The old Sussex tortoise, that I have mentioned to you so often, is become my property. I dug it out of its winter dormitory in March last, when it was enough awakened to express its resentments by hissing; and packing it in a box with earth, carried it eighty miles in post-chaises. The rattle and hurry of the journey so perfectly roused it that, when I turned it out on a border, it walked twice down to the bottom of my garden; however, in the evening, the weather being cold, it buried itself in the loose mould, and continues still concealed.

As it will be under my eye, I shall now have an opportunity of enlarging my observations on its mode of life, and propensities; and perceive already that towards the time of coming forth, it opens a breathing-place in the ground near its head, requiring, I conclude, a freer respiration as it becomes more alive. This creature not only goes under the earth from the middle of November to the middle of April, but sleeps a great part of the summer; for it goes to bed in the longest days at four in the afternoon, and often does not stir in the morning till late. Besides, it retires to rest for every shower; and does not move at all on wet days.

When one reflects on the state of this strange being, it is a matter of wonder to find that Providence should bestow such a profusion of days, such a seeming waste of longevity, on a reptile that appears to relish it so little as to squander more than two-thirds of its existence in a joyless stupor, and be lost to all sensation for months together in the profoundest of slumbers.

While I was writing this letter, a moist and warm afternoon, with the thermometer at fifty, brought forth troops of shell-snails, and, at the same juncture, the tortoise heaved up the mould and put out his head; and the next morning came forth, as it were raised from the dead; and walked about till four in the afternoon. This was a curious coincidence! a very amusing occurrence! to see such a similarity of feelings between the two phereoikoi [house-carriers] for so the Greeks call both the shell-snail and the tortoise.

Because we call "the old family tortoise" an abject reptile, we are too apt to undervalue his abilities, and depreciate his powers of instinct. Yet he is, as Mr. Pope says of his lord,

Much too wise to walk into a well

and has so much discernment as not to fall down a ha-ha: but to stop and withdraw from the brink with the readiest precaution.

Though he loves warm weather, he avoids the hot sun; because his thick shell when once heated, would, as the poet says of solid armor—"scald with safety." He therefore spends the more sultry hours under the umbrella of a large cabbage-leaf, or amidst the waving forests of an asparagus-bed.

But as he avoids heat in the summer, so, in the decline of the year, he improves the faint autumnal beams by getting within the reflection of a fruit-wall; and, though he never has read that planes inclining to the horizon receive a greater share of warmth, he inclines his shell, by tilting it against the wall, to collect and admit every feeble ray.

Pitiable seems the condition of this poor embarrassed reptile: to be cased in a suit of ponderous armor which he cannot lay aside; to be imprisoned, as it were, within his own shell, must preclude, we should suppose, all activity and disposition for enterprise. Yet there is a season of the year (usually the beginning of June) when his exertions are remarkable. He then walks on tiptoe, and is stirring by five in the morning; and, traversing the garden, examines every wicket and interstice in the fences, through which he will escape if possible; and often has eluded the care of the gardener, and wandered to some distant field. The motives that impel him to undertake these rambles seem to be of the amorous kind: his fancy then becomes intent on sexual attachments, which transport him beyond his usual gravity, and induce him to forget for a time his ordinary solemn deportment.

MAYA TURTLE

Antonio Médiz Bolio

The Maya folklorist and intellectual Antonio Médiz Bolio (1884–1945), the translator of the Book of Chilam Balam, *explains the turtle's place in his people's thought.*

Not the air nor the water, nor earth nor fire, frightens the turtle, because it is humble and prudent. This is just the case with the little brilliant turtle of the Maya, the symbol of constancy and purity.

It has four feet with fine white nails. With these it digs into the earth to move itself along, and with these it swims across the lagoons. It goes from place to place, carrying afar silent messages.

When something bad is going to happen, the turtle slips into the shallow water underneath our wells and stays there for several days, until what is going to happen has happened. Then it emerges, clean and beautiful, and it wanders around in the sun, resplendent, raising its red head, with its little round eyes, shining and impenetrable.

Like the good men of ancient times, the turtle, wandering and silent, lives for a hundred and more years.

For all its life and even after death it teaches us sweet and elevated things.

Whoever kills it on purpose commits a great sin before the great spirit above. When it dies on its own, it is all right to make adornments out of its beautiful empty shell, and to place inside it a taut string with which to make holy music.

In the great days of the Maya the turtle was sculpted in the corniches and doors of the temples.

It was like a word from the gods that men once knew how to understand.

translated by Gregory McNamee

A DEAD TURTLE
African-American folktale

In 1925 the folklorist A.W. Eddins collected this story from an African-American turtleman who worked the delta of the Brazos River, in Texas. We preserve the turtleman's idiom, as Eddins recorded it, for the sake of authenticity.

Two young Negroes fishing in the Sumpter Hole came upon a turtle which someone had recently caught and, in order to get the hook out of its mouth, had drawn its head out of the shell and cut it off, leaving the turtle on the ground. The turtle, of course, does not die until sundown, and so it was still floundering around when the Negroes passed by.

One of the Negroes said, "Dar's er daid turkle."

The other looked and replied, "Boy, you is foolish. Dat ar turkle ain't daid."

"Course he's daid. His haid's done cut off. Anything what's got hits haid cut off's bound ter be daid."

"No, he hadn't daid. He's still er-crawlin'. Er daid thing cain't crawl."

"I'll bet yer er dime he's daid."

"You's faded. Er dime says he ain't daid."

So they argued, and finally decided to leave the matter to Uncle Toby, who was fishing farther down the river and who had the reputation of being a very good judge of small matters. Going down to where Uncle Toby sat on a log, the contestants argued their points at length. A dime was at stake and the decision was important.

The first boy said: "Now, Uncle Toby, you knows dat turkle am daid. Hit's haid is done cut off, en nothin' kin live wid hit's haid off. He's bound ter be daid, en I win dat dime."

Then the other spoke: "Uncle Toby, course dat turkle ain't daid. He's still er-crawlin' erround. Anything that can crawl cain't be daid. Dat's my dime, Uncle Toby, en when I wants hit I wants hit."

Uncle Toby smoked his pipe in silence a long time, while he carefully weighed all the facts in the case; then he gave his decision in slow and carefully chosen words. "Now, boys, hit's jes' like dis. Dat ar turkle is daid but he don't know hit."

TURTLE-CATCHING MEDICINE
Tule Indian song

The Tule Indians of Panama sing this medicine song before hunting turtles.

I am going to shoot a little bird,
Sarwiwisopi, that can tame the turtle,
Now I bring it home and hide it,
Then put it in a little clay stove until it burns to ashes;
I am mixing the ashes with red medicine,
From the juice of a certain tree I make this medicine;
I am cutting a little round gourd in two, cutting off
   the top very neatly,
With my knife I scrape the inside of the gourd,
Scrape it smooth and clean like a cup;
I put the medicine into this cup—
Ashes of the little bird and red tree-juice,
Now I tie the cover on tightly,
Put it in my trunk and tell nobody.

Every night for eight nights I take the gourd out
   of my trunk,
The smooth round gourd, with top tied on so tightly,
I put cocoa beans on a little fire and smoke the gourd,
Singing this song while the smoke curls around it—
"Little bird, I saw you

And I knew you would be a good bird to catch a turtle,
That is why I shot you.
Now if you do not tame the turtle
Everyone will say you are not a good bird,
But I know you will tame the turtle,
Then I will make lots of money
To buy a gun, a shirt, and many things I like."
After the eighth night of singing my partner comes,
We go down to my canoe,
I put the gourd carefully in the middle of the canoe,
I have a long pole, a spearhead and a line,
The spearhead will be fastened on the pole
And with it I will spear the turtle.

Now I am talking to the medicine in the gourd
    and saying,
When we get out to the ocean
l will send you down under the water,
I will send you down to attract the turtle,
When you get to the bottom of the water
You must put on your pretty blue dress
So the turtle will come to you.
Change your dress many times,
If the turtle has on a yellow dress
You must put on a yellow dress,
If the turtle has on a white dress
You must put on a white dress,
If the turtle has on a blue dress
You must put on a blue dress,

You must do this to attract him.
When you get the turtle
Bring him up to the canoe and I will spear him.
Tell the turtle that the man who sent you is not
   going to kill him,
Tell the turtle I will only take off his shell and send
   him back where he came from,
So you will catch many turtles for me,
And everyone will say you are a good bird.

translated by Frances Densmore

THE FRIENDSHIP OF THE TORTOISE AND THE EAGLE
Central African folktale

Tortoises enjoy a relationship with birds of prey in many folkloric traditions, as this African story shows.

The tortoise and the eagle did not often meet, for the eagle spent his days in the clouds and the tortoise stayed under a bush. However, when the eagle heard what a warm-hearted chap the tortoise was, he went to pay a call on him.

The tortoise showed such pleasure in his company and fed him so well that the eagle returned again and again, while every time as he flew away he laughed, "Ha! I can enjoy tortoise's hospitality on the ground, but I never have to repay it in my treetop aerie. He can't reach it!"

The eagle's frequent visits and his ingratitude became the favorite subject of gossip among the forest animals.

The eagle and the frog were never on speaking terms, for the eagle was accustomed to swooping down to carry a frog home for supper. So the frog called from the stream bank, "Tortoise, give me beans to eat and I will give you wisdom." After eating the beans the frog said, "Tortoise, the eagle is taking advantage of your kindness. After every visit he flies away, laughing, 'Ha! I can enjoy tortoise's hospitality on the ground, but he can never enjoy mine, for my aerie is in the treetops, and he can't reach it.' Next time the eagle visits you, say, 'Give me a gourd, and I will send food to your wife and children too.'"

As tortoise asked, on his next visit the eagle brought a gourd. After feasting he said, "I'll come back for my wife's meal."

The eagle flew away, laughing to himself as usual, "Ha! I have enjoyed that tortoise's food, but he can never come to my aerie to taste mine."

The frog arrived and said, "Now, tortoise, get into the gourd. The eagle will carry you to his home in the treetops."

Soon the eagle returned. The tortoise's wife told him, "My husband is away, but he left this gourd filled with food for your family."

The eagle flew away with the gourd, not knowing that the tortoise was inside.

The tortoise could hear every word as the eagle laughed, "Ha! I share the tortoise's food but he can never visit my aerie to share mine."

When the eagle's wife emptied the gourd out onto the table, the tortoise crawled out and said, "Friend eagle, you have so often visited my home that I thought it would be nice to visit yours."

The eagle was furious. "I will claw the flesh from your bones," he said. But he broke his talons on the tortoise's shell.

"You're not much of a friend, threatening to tear me limb from limb," said the tortoise. "Please take me home, now that we're no longer friends." "Take you home!" cried the eagle. "I'll throw you to the ground and smash you to pieces!" But at that, the tortoise bit the eagle's leg.

"Let go, let go, let go," the eagle cried.

"I will when you take me home," said the tortoise.

The eagle flew high into the clouds and darted down as fast as an arrow. He shook his leg. He turned and twirled, but it was no use. He could not get the tortoise to relax his grip.

He took the tortoise home. As the eagle flew off, the tortoise called after him, "Friendship requires two people to share their love and their possessions. Because you feel that you can abuse my hospitality, you do not need to call on me again."

SNAPPER

Franklin Burroughs

*In this combination of naturalistic observation and memoir, Frank-
lin Burroughs shows us that turtles carry sentiments as well as
shells on their backs.*

On this Tuesday morning in Maine, with the fields full of
flowers and late June imitating early May ... as I started out
down the gravel road that connects our house to the highway, and drew abreast of the little quarter-acre pond that sits
to the left of the road, here was, large as life and squarely in
my way, a big mama snapping turtle, excavating herself a
hole to lay her eggs in. I was in no particular hurry, and so
I stopped and got out to investigate. Snappers are the most
widely distributed of North American turtles, and they are
by no means uncommon in Maine, but they are normally
reclusive, and when one makes a public appearance it is not
an event to be passed over lightly. This particular one certainly had no intention of being passed over lightly—if she
had intended to blockade the road, she couldn't have chosen a better spot.

Several things distinguish them from other freshwater
turtles, most obviously their size. The one at my feet was
about two feet long, from the tip of her snout to the tip of
her tail. When I eventually picked her up by the tail (and
that is another distinguishing feature of snapping turtles—
you pick up an ordinary turtle by the rim of its shell, but

a snapper's neck is remarkably long and flexible, so you grab the creature by the tail and hold it well out from your body), I guessed she weighed a good twenty pounds.

The general proportions of a snapping turtle are wrong. The head is far too big; the shell is too little. The plastron, or undershell, is ridiculously skimpy—it seems barely adequate for the purposes of decency, and as useless as a bikini would be as far as anatomical protection is concerned. Consequently a snapper cannot withdraw into itself as other turtles do. It retracts the head enough to shield its neck and doesn't even attempt to pull in its legs and feet. The legs and tail are large in relation to the body. When a snapper decides to walk it really walks, the bottom of the shell is a couple of inches off the ground, and, with its dorsally tuberculate tail, long claws, and wickedly hooked beak, it looks like a scaled-down stegosaur.

A snapper compensates for its inadequate armor in a variety of ways, the most immediately apparent of which is athletic ability combined with a very bad temper. It can whirl and lunge ferociously, and if turned over on its back, can, with a thrust and twist of its mighty neck, be upright and ready for mayhem. If you approach one out of water, it opens its mouth and hisses; if you get closer, it lurches at you with such vehemence that it lifts itself off the ground, its jaws snapping savagely at empty air. Archie Carr, whose venerable *Handbook to Turtles* (1952) is the only authority on these matters I possess, states that the disposition to strike is innate, and has been observed in hatchlings "not yet altogether free of their eggshells." An adult can strike, he reports, "with the speed and power of a big rattlesnake." Although Carr does not explicitly say so, the snapper appears to be one of those animals, like the hognose snake, that makes the most of its resemblance to a poisonous snake. Its pale mouth gapes open like a moccasin's, and its aggressiveness involves a certain exaggerated and theatrical posturing. Its official name specifically and subspecifically suggests the highly unturtlelike impression that this creates: *Chelydra serpentina serpentina*. But the snapper, unlike the hognose, can back up its bluff. Its first-strike capability isn't lethal, but it isn't trivial either. According to boyhood folklore, a snapper can bite a broomstick in two, but I have seen the experiment conducted. It took a great deal of goading to persuade the turtle to seize the broomstick at all—it plainly would have preferred the hand that held it—but it finally took it, held it, and crushed and pulped it. Mama's broom handle came out looking like a piece of chewed-over sugarcane. Putting your hand in range of a big snapper would not be like putting it under a guillotine or ax; it would be more like putting it under a bulldozer— a slow, complete crunching.

The shell and skin are a muddy gray; the eye, too, is of a murky mud color. The pupil is black and shaped like a star or a spoked wheel. Within the eye there is a strange yellowish glint, as though you were looking down into turbid water and seeing, in the depths of the water, light from a smoldering fire. It is one of Nature's more nightmarish eyes. The eyes of dragonflies are also nightmarish, but in a different way—they look inhuman, like something out of science fiction. The same is true of the eyes of sharks. The snapper's eye is dull, like a pig's, but inside it there is this savage malevolence, something suggesting not only an evil intention toward the world, but the torment of an inner affliction. Had Milton seen one, he would have associated it with the baleful eye of Satan, an eye reflecting some internal hell of liquid fire, even in Paradise or here on a soft June day, with the bobolinks fluttering aloft and singing in the fields. Snapping turtles did in fact once inhabit Europe, but they died out by the end of the Pleistocene, and so were unknown to what we think of as European history. But they look, nevertheless, like something that Europeans had half-imagined or dimly remembered even before they came to the New World and saw them for the first time. A snapper would do for a gargoyle, or a grotesque parody of a knight on his horse, a thing of armored evil.

Snappers feed on about anything, dead or alive fish, flesh, or fowl. The fish they catch by luring them into range with their vermiform tongues, which may have something to do with the role of trickster that they assume in the mythology of North American Indians. But they can also be caught in a trap baited with bananas. They are not fastidious: Schmidt and Inger (1957) tell the gruesome story of an elderly man who used a tethered snapping turtle to recover the bodies of people who had drowned. We do not learn what this sinister gentleman fed his useful pet to encourage its predilection for water-logged cadavers. I know on my own authority that snappers are death on ducks, and will rise like a shadow from the cozy muck of the bottom, under the jocund and unsuspecting drake as it briskly preens and putters on the surface of the pond, lock sudden jaws around one suspended leg, one webbed foot, and sink quietly back to the depths, their weight too much for the duck to resist, their jaws a functional illustration of necessity's sharp pinch. There in the darkness the duck is ponderously mauled, mutilated, and eaten, right down to the toenails. We watched a hen mallard and a brood of ducklings disappear from the little pond beside the road one summer—two or three inexplicable deductions per week—until at last only the very nervous hen and one trusting little duckling remained. Then there was only the duckling. It peeped and chirped and swam distractedly around the pond in a most heart-rending fashion. I tried to trap it so we could rear it in confinement and safety, but there was no catching it, and the next day it was gone too.

The law of tooth and nail is all right with me when it involves hawks and mice, or foxes and geese, or even sharks and swimmers—there is a redeeming elegance in most predators, a breathtaking speed and agility. If I thought I could tempt an eagle to stoop, I'd gladly stake my best laying hen in the yard to see it happen. But a snapper is an ugly proposition, more like cancer than a crab is. If one grabs your finger, you do not get the finger back—that too is boyhood folklore, but I have never tested it. Some propositions call for implicit faith, even in these post-theological and deconstructing days.

Unlike most of the other freshwater turtles, snappers never emerge to bask on rocks or logs. They come out in late spring or early summer; their emergence here coincides with the vetch, the stitchwort, bedstraw, and hawkweed. They need sandy soil to lay their eggs in, and such soil isn't always close to the sorts of boggy, miry waters they inhabit. They will often go overland a surprising distance. Even so, Carr says that females will sometimes cross large areas of suitable terrain before finally deciding on a spot to dig. He waxes jocosely sociobiological: "This characteristic ... may be seen in most nesting turtles and may indeed be homologous to the traditional urge in the human female to move the furniture about."

Roadbeds and railway embankments can provide good sites that are reasonably convenient to their usual habitats. Creatures of darkness, cursing the light, they lumber up from pond or river, and one morning you awake to the frantic yapping of dogs and go out, and there, foul and hissing, like some chieftain of the underworld at last summoned to justice and surrounded by reporters and cameras, stands a great gravid snapper. The flesh of her neck, legs, and tail—all the parts that ought to fit inside the shell but don't—has, on the underside, a grimy yellowish cast to it, is podgy, lewd, wrinkled, and soft. In Maine there will nominally be one or two big leeches hanging onto the nether parts. These portions of the animal seem to have no proper covering—no scales, feathers, hair, or taut, smooth epidermis. It looks as though the internal anatomy had been extruded, or the whole animal plucked or flayed.

I'm not sure how much of this natural history Ricky McIver and I understood when we were nine or ten; we only knew that, trekking down a sandy road in midsummer, we would suddenly come upon a baby snapper, bustling along with remarkable purpose, as though on its way to catch a train. Of course we would catch the turtle, and one of us would take it home and put it in a dishpan with some water and keep it under the bed, where all night long there would be the tinny scraping of little claws, as the turtle went round and round inside the pan. Sometimes one would escape, instigating a general panicky search of the room and the house. It would turn up far back under a sofa or cabinet, covered with dust and weakened by dehydration, but still able to muster a parched snap and hiss. Finally we would let it go into a drainage ditch. We never came upon a mother laying her eggs—given the heat, perhaps they did that at night down south. Up here I seem to come across one or two of them every year, and have learned to look for them along road shoulders in late June.

∾

I backed the car up to the house to get Susan and Hannah—the older girls were still asleep—and our old pointer Jacob roused himself and walked down with us, conferring by his stiff-jointed, wheezing Nestorian solemnity an air of officialdom upon the occasion, as though we were a commission sent out to investigate an unregistered alien that had showed up in Bowdoinham. Hannah went along grudgingly, with a five-year-old's saving sense that any time the parents promised to show you something interesting, they probably had concealed motives of one sort or another. When we got to the turtle, Jacob hoisted his hackles, clapped his tail between his legs, and circled her a few times, then sat down and barked once. The turtle raised herself on her forelegs, head up, mouth agape; her hostility did not focus on any one of us so much as on the whole situation in which she found herself. Hannah looked at all of this and pronounced it boring; could she have a friend over to play? The dog seemed to feel that he had discharged his obligations by barking, and shambled over to the edge of the field, pawed fretfully at the ground, then settled himself, curled up, sighed, and went to sleep. The whole thing was beginning to take on the unpromising aspect of Nature Study, an ersatz experience.

We walked around behind the turtle, and there did make a discovery of sorts. Through all of the commotion that surrounded her anterior end, her hind legs were methodically digging. Their motion was impressively regular and mechanical: first one leg thrust down into the hole, then the other, smooth and steady as pistons. Whatever the snapper felt or thought about her situation plainly did not concern the legs, which were wholly intent on procreation. It seemed an awkward way to dig, the hind foot being a clumsy and inflexible instrument anyway, and having to carry on its operations huggermugger like that, out of sight and out of mind too, if the turtle could be said to have a mind. We could not see down into the hole, only the legs alternately reaching down, and a rim of excavated sand that was slowly growing up behind the rim of the turtle's shell. I was later to learn that the digging action, once begun, is as involuntary as the contractions of a mammal giving birth, and even a turtle missing one hind leg will dig in the same fashion, thrusting down first with the good leg, then with the amputated stump, until the job is done.

Hannah, an aficionado of the sandbox, permitted herself a cautious interest in this end of the turtle's operations, and wanted to inspect her hole. I wasn't sure about the ethics of this. It is a general law that you don't disturb nesting creatures; it was, after all, no fault of the snapper's if she failed to excite in us the veneration that generally attaches to scenes of maternity and nativity. On the other hand, she had chosen a bad place. I could see where my neighbor Gene Hamrick had carefully driven around her, going well over onto the shoulder to do so. Other neighbors might be less considerate, and the nest itself would, in any event, be packed hard by the traffic in a few weeks, rendering the future of the eggs and hatchlings highly uncertain. So I grasped her tail and hoisted her up. Aloft, she held herself rigidly spread-eagle, her head and neck parallel to the earth, and hissed mightily as I took her over and put her in the little ditch that drains the pond. Because of the recent rain, the ditch was flowing, and as soon as her front feet touched the water, all of her aggression ceased, and she seemed bent on nothing but escape. She had surprising power as she scrabbled at the banks and bottom of the ditch; it was like holding onto a miniature bulldozer. I let her go and she surged off down the ditch, head submerged and carapace just awash. She stopped once and raised her head and fixed us with her evil eye; the mouth dropped open in a last defiance. Then she lowered her head again and waddled out of sight.

TURTLE AND WOLF
Alabama-Coushatta folktale

Turtle is a trickster in many traditions around the world—but usually one who trips himself up at every turn.

One day some wolves chased a fawn. The fawn soon became exhausted, so it jumped into the fork of a hickory tree. The wolves could not get the fawn down, and they ran around and around the tree in frustration.

Turtle came along and found the wolves in council. "What are you talking about?" he asked.

"A fawn is up in that tree, and we are trying to get it down," one of the wolves said.

Turtle said he would help. He killed the fawn with his bow and arrow.

The chief of the wolves asked, "What part do you want? The leg? or the shoulder?"

"No, I don't want any of the meat," Turtle replied. The wolves then set upon the carcass and ate it up.

After the wolves had left, Turtle decided to play a trick on his wife. He took some of the fawn's blood and wrapped leaves around it. He put the roll on his back and went home. Turtle said to his wife, "This is fresh venison."

His wife untied the bundle but found only leaves. She grew angry and threw the blood into Turtle's eyes. That is why they are red.

THE TORTOISE AND
THE PEACOCKS
Julian Ursyn Niemcewicz

Eighteenth-century Polish political fables often depict the downfall of the kingdom through animal figures. In this instance, the poet Julian Ursyn Niemcewicz (1758–1841) lampoons the aspirations of the peacock-proud nobility and the long-suffering peasantry.

Grand in their display,
Two peacocks strolled among the courtyard fowl.
They flashed their agile tails,
Dazzling azure, emerald and gold.
Lo and behold, one morning,
Standing side by side,
And I don't know what they were thinking,
There occurred an abrupt quaking,
Causing great amazement.
Out of curiosity and fear,
With their heads bent to the ground,
Their tails open to their beaks,
They took a look.
The beast who roused such resplendent alarm
Was a torpid tortoise,
Who, as if sobbing the tale of the nation's woes,
Had considered deeply for the last two years
Whether to stay in the pond or to surface.
In the end he showed himself,

But his ungainly stance
Drew the gaze of the boundless peacocks.
Our tortoise joined nobility to stupidity
By sticking his neck out,
Glancing in every direction a hundred times,
Displaying one limb,
And after much musing bringing it forward,
And then, a second limb.
Again, he reflected and pondered until, after all,
He recognized it was necessary to bring forward the third.
In the end he supposed this unparalleled truth:
"If I don't move the fourth, I'll stay right here."
So he moved in small progressive steps,
And the peacocks after him with their tails and eyes open,
Strutting and wondering: "What will come of this?
The wisest of the animal family is surely the tortoise;
See his dignity, discernment, purpose and heed;
If he is this cautious at every hazard,
The objective of his journey must be grand indeed."
But the peacocks guessed wrong; for all his toil,
All his calm and consideration,
Where did our tortoise find himself?
Behold! In the mud.

translated by Liliana Slomkowska

TWO FABLES
Aesop

Of all the stories told about turtles the world over, these ancient Greek fables are universally the best known, translated into countless languages and adapted by many cultures.

1

A tortoise, after lazing in the sun all day long, complained to a flock of sea birds that no one would teach her to fly. An eagle, hovering nearby, heard her and asked what she would give him if he would take her aloft. "I will give you all the riches of the Red Sea," she replied. "All right, then," the eagle said, "I will teach you to fly." Grabbing her with his sharp talons, he carried her up until they brushed the clouds. Suddenly he let her go, and she fell onto the rocky slope of a tall mountain, breaking her shell to bits. As the eagle swooped in to feast upon her, the tortoise cried, "I deserve this end! What business do I have traveling among the clouds when I move about on the earth so slowly?"

2

One day a hare ridiculed the short feet and slow movements of a tortoise, who replied, "You may think that you're as swift as the wind, but I promise you, I'll win in a race against you." The hare took the tortoise up on the bet. The two started off together. The tortoise kept on plodding along, not once stopping, at a slow and steady pace to the end of the course. The hare, lying down on a soft patch of grass to catch its breath, fell fast asleep. When he awoke, he saw the tortoise crossing the finish line far ahead.

translated by Gregory McNamee

HOW THE TERRAPIN BEAT THE RABBIT
Cherokee folktale

This Cherokee story, collected by the folklorist Harold Mooney in the 1890s, is probably an adaptation of the previous Aesopian fable, although it introduces some unmistakably Native American elements.

The Rabbit was a great runner, and everybody knew it. No one thought the Terrapin anything but a slow traveler, but he was a great warrior and very boastful, and the two were always disputing about their speed. At last they agreed to decide the matter by a race. They fixed the day and the starting place and arranged to run across four mountain ridges, and the one who came in first at the end was to be the winner.

The Rabbit felt so sure of it that he said to the Terrapin, "You know you can't run. You can never win the race, so I'll give you the first ridge and then you'll have only three to cross while I go over four."

The Terrapin said that would be all right, but that night when he went home to his family he sent for his Terrapin friends and told them he wanted their help. He said he knew he could not outrun the Rabbit, but he wanted to stop the Rabbit's boasting. He explained his plan to his friends and they agreed to help him.

When the day came all the animals were there to see the race. The Rabbit was with them, but the Terrapin was gone ahead toward the first ridge, as they had arranged, and they could hardly see him on account of the long grass. The word was given and the Rabbit started off with long jumps up the mountain, expecting to win the race before the Terrapin could get down the other side. But before he got up the mountain he saw the Terrapin go over the ridge ahead of him. He ran on, and when he reached the top he looked all around, but could not see the Terrapin on account of the long grass. He kept on down the mountain and began to climb the second ridge, but when he looked up again there was the Terrapin just going over the top. Now he was surprised and made his longest jumps to catch up, but when he got to the top there was the Terrapin away in front going over the third ridge. The Rabbit was getting tired now and nearly out of breath, but he kept on down the mountain and up the other ridge until he got to the top just in time to see the Terrapin cross the fourth ridge and thus win the race.

The Rabbit could not make another jump, but fell over on the ground, crying *mi, mi, mi, mi*, as the Rabbit does ever since when he is too tired to run any more. The race was given to the Terrapin and all the animals wondered how he could win against the Rabbit, but he kept still and never told. It was easy enough, however, because all the Terrapin's friends looked just alike, and he had simply posted one near the top of each ridge to wait until the Rabbit came in sight and then climb over and hide in the long grass. When the Rabbit came on he could not find the Terrapin and so thought the Terrapin was ahead, and if he had met one of the other terrapins he would have thought it the same one because they looked so much alike. The real Terrapin had posted himself on the fourth ridge, so as to come in at the end of the race and be ready to answer questions if the animals suspected anything.

Because the Rabbit had to lie down and lose the race the conjurer now, when preparing his young men for the ball play, boils a lot of rabbit hamstrings into a soup, and sends someone at night to pour it across the path along which the other players are to come in the morning, so that they may become tired in the same way and lose the game. It is not always easy to do this, because the other party is expecting it and has watchers ahead to prevent it.

TORTOISE ON THE HOOF
Edward Lear

Chelonian silliness from the king of silly verse, the Victorian limerickmonger Edward Lear.

> There was an Old Person of Ickley,
> Who could not abide to ride quickly.
> He rode to Karnak on a tortoise's back,
> That moony Old Person of Ickley.

WAYAMBA THE TURTLE

Wagarra (Australian aborigine) folktale

How did turtles come to live in water? This Australian story pro-poses an answer.

Oola the lizard was out getting yams on a mirria flat. She had three of her children with her. Suddenly she thought she heard someone moving behind the big mirria bushes. She listened. All of a sudden out jumped Wayamba from behind a bush and seized Oola, telling her not to make a noise and he would not hurt her, but that he meant to take her off to his camp to be his wife. He would take her three children, too, and look after them.

Resistance was useless, for Oola had only her yam stick, while Wayamba had his spears and boondis. Wayamba took the woman and her children to his camp.

His tribe, when they saw him bring home a woman of the Oola tribe, asked him if her tribe had given her to him. He said, "No, I have stolen her."

"Well," they said, "her tribe will soon be after her. You must protect yourself, we shall not fight for you. You had no right to steal her without telling us. We had a young woman of our own tribe for you, yet you go and steal an Oola and bring her to the camp of the Wayambas. On your own head be the consequences."

In a short time the Oolas were seen coming across the plain which faced the camp of the Wayambas. And they came not in friendship or to parley, for no women were with them. They carried no boughs of peace in their hands, but were painted as for war, and were armed with fighting weapons.

When all the Wayambas saw the approach of the Oolas, their wise man said, "Now, Wayamba, you had better go out on the plain and do your own fighting. We shall not help you."

Wayamba chose the two biggest boreens, or shields, that he had. One he slung on him, covering the front of his body, and one the back. Then, seizing his weapons, he strode out to meet his enemies.

When he was well out onto the plain, though still some distance from the Oolas, he called out, "Come on."

The answer was a shower of spears and boomerangs. As they came whizzing through the air Wayamba drew his arms inside the boreens, ducked his head down between them and so escaped.

As the weapons fell harmless to the ground, glancing off his boreen, out again he stretched his arms and held up again his head, shouting, "Come on, try again, I'm ready."

The answer was another shower of weapons, which he met in the same way. At last the Oolas closed in around him, forcing him to retreat toward the creek.

Shower after shower of weapons they slung at him, and were getting at such close quarters that his only chance was to dive into the creek. He turned toward the creek, tore the front boreen off him, flung down his weapons and plunged in.

The Oolas waited, spears poised in hand, ready to aim the moment his head appeared above water, but they waited in vain.

Wayamba the blackfellow they never saw again. But in the water hole wherein he had dived they saw a strange creature, which bore on its back a fixed plate like a boreen. When they went to try and catch the creature it drew in its head and limbs. So they said, "It is Wayamba."

And this was the beginning of Wayamba, or turtle, in the creeks.

retold by K. Langloh Parker

THE PLOWSHARE TURTLES OF MADAGASCAR

Gerald Durrell

Even turtles, the famed zoologist Gerald Durrell suggests, fall in love.

The strange protuberance of the shell under the head (which bestows on it the name plowshare) is the animal's fighting gear. It is essential, apparently, for the males to fight in order to be roused to such a pitch that they are overcome with emotion and can mate with the females.

A lone male kept with any number of luscious, buxom and voluptuous females (by tortoise standards) just tends to wander round forlornly, ignoring the wiles and manifold attractions of the females, simply because he has no one to fight. To be the only male, surrounded by attractive and willing females, is a situation, you would have thought, that would bring out the Don Juan in any tortoise worth his salt, but the plowshare needs fisticuffs as an aphrodisiac. When the situation is right, however, battle commences and it is a fascinating contest to watch.

The two males, round as Tweedledum and Tweedledee dressed for battle, approach each other at what, for a tortoise, is a smart trot. The shells clash together and then the plowshare comes into use. Each male struggles to get this projection beneath his opponent and overturn him to win a victory in this bloodless duel. They stagger to and fro like scaly sumo wrestlers, the dust kicked up into little clouds around them, while the subject of their adoration gazes at their passionate endeavors, showing about as much excitement and enthusiasm as a plum pudding.

Finally, one or the other of the suitors gets his weapon in the right position and skidding along and heaving madly, he at last overturns his opponent. Then, he turns and lumbers over to gain his just reward from the female, while the vanquished tortoise, with much leg-waving and effort, rights himself and wanders dispiritedly away. Like so many battles in nature, it is merely a stimulus, a trial of strength in which no one is hurt and no gore is shed.

The actual mating process begins with the male turning the female over a couple of times, perhaps to keep her humble after the potentially ego-inspiring battle for her attention, and culminates with the big event, which will hopefully result in the propagation of this species, the world's most threatened reptile.

TWO TURTLE TUNES
Akimel O'odham folksongs

In the traditional belief of the Akimel O'odham people of southern Arizona, to impede a turtle's progress over the desert is to invite disaster and sickness, especially infirmities of the legs. The anthropologist Frank Russell recorded these Akimel O'odham turtle songs in 1901.

1

The Black Turtle now approaches us,
Wearing and shaking his belt of night.
The Black Turtle now approaches us,
Wearing and shaking his belt of night.
The harlot arose and ran about,
Beating her breast and the air.
The harlot arose and ran about,
Beating her breast and the air.
Understand, my younger brothers,
That it is the Sun that gives me
The trance vision that I see.
The Sun gives magic power.

2

Turtle, Turtle, where are you?
Where is the pond in which you swim?
Kosta, kosta, kosta, kosta,
Where is the water you swim in?

THE LEOPARD TORTOISE
Bushman folktale

Willem Bleek, a folklorist, learned this strange report on the habits of Testudo pardalis, *the leopard tortoise, from a South African Bushman elder in the early 1900s. In this tale, whose meaning is not transparent, the tortoise starts off as a human woman but shifts shape without the narrator's telling us quite how.*

The people had gone hunting: she was ill; and she perceived a man who came up to her hut; he had been hunting around.

She asked the man to rub her neck a little with fat for her; for, it ached. The man rubbed it with fat for her. And she held the man firmly with the muscles of her neck. The man's hands altogether decayed away in it.

She spied another man, who came hunting. And she also spoke, she said: "Rub me with fat a little."

And the man whose hands had decayed away in her neck, he was hiding his hands, so that the other man should not perceive them, namely, that they had decayed away in it. And he said; "Yes; O my mate! rub our elder sister a little with fat; for the moon has been cut, while our elder sister lies ill. Thou shalt also rub our elder sister with fat." He was hiding his hands, so that the other one should not perceive them.

The Leopard Tortoise said: "Rubbing with fat, put thy hands into my neck." And he, rubbing with fat, put in his hands upon the Leopard Tortoise's neck; and the Leopard Tortoise drew in her head upon her neck; while his hands were altogether in her neck; and he dashed the Leopard Tortoise upon the ground, on account of it; while he desired, he thought, that he should, by dashing it upon the ground, break the Leopard Tortoise. And the Leopard Tortoise held him fast.

The other one had taken out his hands from behind his back; and he exclaimed: "Feel thou that which I did also feel!" and he showed the other one his hands; and the other one's hands were altogether inside the Leopard Tortoise's neck. And he arose, he returned home. And the other one was dashing the Leopard Tortoise upon the ground; while he returning went; and he said that the other one also felt what he had felt. A pleasant thing it was not, in which he had been! He yonder returning went; he arrived at home.

The people exclaimed: "Where hast thou been?" And he, answering, said that the Leopard Tortoise had been the one in whose neck his hands had been; that was why he had not returned home. The people said: "Art thou a fool? Did not thy parents instruct thee? The Leopard Tortoise always seems as if she would die; while she is deceiving us."

ANCIENT KNOWLEDGE
Aelian

Writing in Greek in the second century A.D., *the Latin poet Aelian gathered wondrous reports of animal behavior in his* On the Characteristics of Animals, *including these notes on the chelonian order.*

Tortoises are a product of Libya. They have a most cruel look, and they live in the mountains, and their shell is good for making lyres.

~

After eating marjoram, the land tortoise treats vipers with contempt. If marjoram is not to be found, then it arms itself by eating rue. If it cannot find either, however, it is killed.

~

The river turtle of India has a shell as big as a full-sized skiff. Each one can hold about 120 gallons of pulse. There are also land-tortoises there, and these may be the size of the large clods of dirt that get turned up during deep plowing. These tortoises, it is said, shed their covering. The plowmen who work in the fields dig them out with sticks as if they were grubs. The flesh of tortoises is sweet and fat, and is by no means bitter, like that of the turtle.

~

Eagles seize tortoises and dash them onto the rocks from on high. Then they soar down and eat the flesh out of the broken shell. It was in this way, I am told, that Aeschylus, the great tragedian, met his death. Aeschylus was sitting on a rock, thinking about something and writing. He was bald. An eagle, thinking that his head was a rock, dropped a tortoise on him. The tortoise killed the poet.

~

In the Indian Ocean lives a sea-turtle that is huge, and people make roofs out of their shells, so that many people can live under just one of them. This keeps out the fiery sun and wards off the most awful downpours of rain. These people have no need to replace broken tiles, as they would with a normal roof, because the turtle's shell is hard and resembles a rock that has been pitted, like the roof of a cave.

~

A turtle, even with its head cut off, will close its eyes if you bring your hand near. But if you bring it too near, it will bite you. It has eyes that glint and flash from a long way away, the pupils being pure white. When they are removed, these eyes are set in gold pieces and in necklaces, for which reason they are coveted by women. These turtles, I have been told, are natives of the Red Sea region.

~

The land tortoise is a lustful creature, at least the male is. The female, however, mates unwillingly. Demostratus, a member of the Roman Senate—not that this makes him a sufficient authority, though he knew all there was to know about fishing and was a fine lecturer on the subject, and I would not be surprised if he has studied much weightier subjects, such as the science of the soul—admits that he does not know whether there is any other reason for the female's declining to copulate, but he offers this fact. The female couples only when looking towards the male, and when he has satisfied himself he lumbers away, while the female is quite unable to turn over again owing to the bulk of her shell and because she has been pressed into the ground. And so she is abandoned by her mate to provide a meal for other animals, especially eagles. This, Demostratus says, is what the females fear most, and because their desires are modest and they prefer life to pleasure, the males are unable to coax them to the act of copulation. And so by some mysterious instinct the males cast an amorous spell that brings forgetfulness of all fear. It seems that the spells of a tortoise in loving mood are by no means songs, like the trifles that Theocritus wrote, but a mysterious herb of which Demostratus admits that neither he nor anyone else knows the name. Apparently the males adorn themselves with this herb, and something mysterious occurs. At any rate, if they hold this herb in their mouth the exact opposite of what I have been describing occurs: the male becomes coy, but the formerly reluctant female is now full of ardor and runs after him in a frenzied desire to mate.

translated by Gregory McNamee

TWO SIDES TO A TORTOISE
Herman Melville

In The Encantadas *(1854), a journal of sailing in the South Pacific, Herman Melville relates this capture of three tortoises that may well have been first cousins of the ones Charles Darwin describes (see p. 94). As always, Melville puts a philosophical spin on the ways of these unlucky tortoises. "Their crowning curse," he writes, "is their drudging impulse to straightforwardness in a belittered world." We would say their curse is more properly their inability to move quickly enough to escape marauding humans.*

Most ugly shapes and horrible aspects,
Such as Dame Nature selfe mote feare to see,
Or shame, that ever should so fowle defects
From her most cunning hand escaped bee;
All dreadfull pourtraicts of deformitee:
Ne wonder, if these do a man appall;
For all that here at home we dreadfull hold,
Be but as bugs to fearen babes withall,
Compared to the creatures in these isles' entrall.

"Feare nought," then saide the Palmer well aviz'd,
"For these same monsters are not these in deed,
But are into these fearfull shapes disguiz'd."
And lifting up his vertuous staffe on bye,
Then all that dreadfull armie fast can flye
Into great Tethys bosome, where they hidden lye.

In view of the description given, may one be gay upon the Encantadas? Yes: that is, find one the gaiety, and he will be gay. And, indeed, sackcloth and ashes as they are, the isles are not perhaps unmitigated gloom. For while no spectator can deny their claims to a most solemn and superstitious consideration, no more than my firmest resolutions can decline to behold the spectre-tortoise when emerging from its shadowy recess; yet even the tortoise, dark and melancholy as it is upon the back, still possesses a bright side; its calipee or breast-plate being sometimes of a faint yellowish or golden tinge. Moreover, everyone knows that tortoises as well as turtles are of such a make, that if you but put them on their backs you thereby expose their bright sides without the possibility of their recovering themselves, and turning into view the other. But after you have done this, and because you have done this, you should not swear that the tortoise has no dark side. Enjoy the bright, keep it turned up perpetually if you can, but be honest, and don't deny the black. Neither should he, who cannot turn the tortoise from its natural position so as to hide the darker and expose his livelier aspect, like a great October pumpkin in the sun, for that cause declare the creature to be one total inky blot. The tortoise is both black and bright. But let us to particulars.

Some months before my first stepping ashore upon the group, my ship was cruising in its close vicinity. One noon we found ourselves off the South Head of Albermarle, and not very far from the land. Partly by way of freak, and partly by way of spying out so strange a country, a boat's crew was sent ashore, with orders to see all they could, and besides, bring back whatever tortoises they could conveniently transport.

It was after sunset, when the adventurers returned. I looked down over the ship's high side as if looking down over the curb of a well, and dimly saw the damp boat deep in the sea with some unwonted weight. Ropes were dropt over, and presently three huge antediluvian-looking tortoises, after much straining, were landed on deck. They seemed hardly of the seed of earth. We had been abroad upon the waters for five long months, a period amply sufficient to make all things of the land wear a fabulous hue to the dreamy mind. Had three Spanish custom-house officers boarded us then, it is not unlikely that I should have curiously stared at them, felt of them, and stroked them much as savages serve civilized guests. But instead of three custom-house officers, behold these really wondrous tortoises—none of your schoolboy mud-turtles—but black as widower's weeds, heavy as chests of plate, with vast shells medallioned and orbed like shields, and dented and blistered like shields that have breasted a battle, shaggy, too, here and there, with dark green moss, and slimy with the spray of the sea. These mystic creatures, suddenly translated by night from unutterable solitudes to our peopled deck, affected me in a manner not easy to unfold. They seemed newly crawled forth from beneath the foundations of the world. Yea, they seemed the identical tortoises whereon the Hindoo plants this total sphere. With a lantern I inspected them more closely. Such worshipful venerableness of aspect! Such furry greenness mantling the rude peelings and healing the fissures of their shattered shells. I no more saw three tortoises. They expanded—became transfigured. I seemed to see three Roman Coliseums in magnificent decay.

Ye oldest inhabitants of this, or any other isle, said I, pray, give me the freedom of your three walled towns.

The great feeling inspired by these creatures was that of age:—dateless, indefinite endurance. And, in fact, that any other creature can live and breathe as long as the tortoise of the Encantadas, I will not readily believe. Not to hint of their known capacity of sustaining life, while going without food for an entire year, consider that impregnable armor of their living mail. What other bodily being possesses such a citadel wherein to resist the assaults of Time?

As lantern in hand, I scraped among the moss and beheld the ancient scars of bruises received in many a sullen fall among the marly mountains of the isle—scars strangely widened, swollen, half obliterate, and yet distorted like those sometimes found in the bark of very hoary trees, I seemed an antiquary of a geologist, studying the bird-tracks and ciphers upon the exhumed slates trod by incredible creatures whose very ghosts are now defunct.

As I lay in my hammock that night, overhead I heard the slow weary draggings of the three ponderous strangers along the encumbered deck. Their stupidity or their resolution was so great, that they never went aside for any impediment. One ceased his movements altogether just before the mid-watch. At sunrise I found him butted like a battering-ram against the immovable foot of the foremast, and still striving, tooth and nail, to force the impossible passage. That these tortoises are the victims of a penal, or malignant, or perhaps a downright diabolical enchanter, seems in nothing more likely than in that strange infatuation of hopeless toil which so often possesses them. I have known them in their journeyings to ram themselves heroically against rocks, and long abide there, nudging, wriggling, wedging, in order to displace them, and so hold on their inflexible path. Their crowning curse is their drudging impulse to straightforwardness in a belittered world.

Meeting with no such hinderance as their companion did, the other tortoises merely fell foul of small stumbling-blocks—buckets, blocks, and coils of rigging—and at times in the act of crawling over them would slip with an astounding rattle to the deck. Listening to these draggings and concussions, I thought me of the haunt from which they came; an isle full of metallic ravines and gulches, sunk bottomlessly into the hearts of splintered mountains, and covered for many miles with inextricable thickets. I then pictured these three straightforward monsters, century after century, writhing through the shades, grim as blacksmiths; crawling so slowly and ponderously, that not only did toad-stools and all fungous things grow beneath their feet, but a sooty moss sprouted upon their backs. With them I lost myself in volcanic mazes; brushed away endless boughs of rotting thickets; till finally in a dream I found myself sitting cross-legged upon the foremost, a Brahmin similarly mounted upon either side, forming a tripod of foreheads which upheld the universal cope.

Such was the wild nightmare begot by my first impression of the Encantadas tortoise. But next evening, strange to say, I sat down with my shipmates, and made a merry repast from tortoise steaks and tortoise stews; and supper over, out knife, and helped convert the three mighty concave shells into three fanciful soup-tureens, and polished the three flat yellowish calipees into three gorgeous salvers.

WHY THE TORTOISE
HAS A ROUND BACK
Romanian folktale

Moritz Gaster, a folklorist, collected this Romanian etiological, or just-so, tale in the early 1900s.

When God and St. Peter were walking on the earth, one day they made a very long journey, and grew very hungry. Coming to a little hut, they found the woman in, and they asked her for something to eat. "Well," she said, "I have very little flour in the house, but I am going to bake two loaves, and when you come back in half an hour they will be ready and you will be welcome to one." Taking the flour, she kneaded it in the trough and made two loaves, one for herself and one for the travelers.

Meanwhile they went to church, but they said before going that they would come back at the end of the service.

The woman covered over the dough, and to her great astonishment, when she lifted the cover, the dough of the loaf for the strangers had risen much higher than the other. Then she put both loaves in the oven. How great was her surprise, on taking out the loaves from the oven, when she found that the one for the travelers had been baked nicely and was a very big loaf, while the one for herself was half burned and almost shriveled to a pancake. When she saw the miracle her greed overtook her, and she forgot the promise which she had made to the travelers.

She said to herself: "Why should I give my best bread to strangers whom I do not know? Let them go elsewhere to richer people than I am."

So she took the pasteboard and put it on the floor, and crouching on it, covered herself over with the trough. She told her little girl to stand in front of the door, and if two old people should come and ask for her she was to say that her mother had gone away and that she did not know where she was. The travelers then, of course, would not come in, and she would be able to enjoy the loaf.

After a while God and St. Peter came back from church, and asked the little girl where her mother was, to which the child replied as she had been told. God said, "Where she is there shall she remain," and went away. The child came in and tried to lift the trough off the back of her mother, who was lying hidden underneath, but try as hard as she could the trough would not come off. It had grown on to the back of her mother, and the pasteboard had grown underneath on to her. The woman was only able to put out her little head with the glistening, greedy eyes, and her tiny little hands and feet, and the handle of the pasteboard had turned into a waggling tail.

And that is how the tortoise was made, when the old woman became the tortoise always carrying the trough and the pasteboard with her.

DESERT TORTOISES
John Cloudsley-Thompson

Writing in Natural History *magazine, the English biologist John Cloudsley-Thompson describes the still-mysterious processes by which desert tortoises keep themselves cool in the heat of day.*

Abdel Gadir was the first of my baby African spurred tortoises and I treasured him accordingly. Thirty years ago, when I taught zoology at the University of Khartoum, we kept a number of these desert tortoises, the world's largest mainland species. (Only the Galapagos and Indian Ocean island giant tortoises can top them.) In November 1965, one of our females laid seventeen eggs, of which only one hatched the following June. Our Sudanese laboratory staff named the baby Abdel Gadir, or "servant of God" in Arabic—a common nickname for tortoises.

Until we could make a proper enclosure, I used to put him on the lawn to graze on the small, succulent shrubs that he evidently preferred to the grass that his parents ate. In order not to lose him, I confined him beneath a clear plastic microscope cover in the shade of a palm tree. One day, on my way home to lunch, I remembered that I had forgotten about Abdel Gadir. I dashed back to find that the sun had moved and he was no longer in the shade! Indeed, the poor little creature was extremely hot, and frothing all over his head and neck. I took him into the laboratory, gave him a drink, and went back to lunch. On the way, a thought struck me. When jerboas and kangaroo rats get overheated, they salivate onto their throats; this cools them and can prolong their life, in an emergency, for up to thirty minutes. (Small mammals cannot afford to cool themselves by sweating and do not possess sweat glands.) Could tortoises respond in a similar way?

The next day, Abdel Gadir found himself in an incubator at 131° F. He was removed every thirty minutes to be weighed and have his body temperature taken. During the first hour, his weight decreased only slightly but his temperature rose from an initial 77° F to 105° F. At this point, Abdel Gadir began to salivate and froth at the mouth; his temperature stabilized, but he began to lose weight rapidly. After another hour, I took him out and gave him a drink of water. He soon recovered and seemed to be none the worse for his experience. Spurred tortoises do not normally drink, for they obtain sufficient moisture from their vegetable food. After salivating, however, Abdel Gadir, and all the other tortoises that I tested, enjoyed a good long drink.

In 1969, I was at the University of New Mexico, in Albuquerque, where physiologist Bud Riedesel, my wife, Anne, and I were testing the responses of ornate box turtles to heat. These turtles also used evaporative cooling— not only by salivating but also by urinating on their back legs. We found that the heartbeat rate increased only when the body temperature increased, but that salivation could be induced by heating the head alone.

If you think that box turtles are pleasant, docile animals to work with, you are mistaken. They have a well-developed hinge midway across the length of the lower shell that enables them to enclose the head and extremities. After a heat-measuring thermocouple was inserted into their rectums a few times, they objected to future tests by snapping their shells closed. If we were not careful, we got our fingers pinched hard. Also, they became exceedingly wary. We had to creep up on them and wedge a cork between their shells to keep them from closing.

That was not the end of their revenge for our experiments in temperature regulation. Like other land turtles and tortoises, the box turtle is endowed with a very large bladder that has several functions. It can be used for emergency cooling, as well as to store water for use during long periods of drought, hibernation, or estivation. But it also emits a foul smell that is an effective deterrent against predators. We soon learned that when picking up a tortoise, you always want to keep its ventral side pointing away from you!

Since our early investigations, a great deal of research has been undertaken on the ways in which tortoises and land turtles of various species regulate their body temperatures. In addition to the considerable insulation provided by their top shells, they cool themselves through salivating and frothing at the mouth, urinating on the back legs, moistening of the eyes, and panting. Another way in which they achieve thermoregulation is by varying the heart rate according to body temperature and by dilating the peripheral blood vessels in response to heating.

Animals can be categorized by the major source of their body heat: endotherms, which warm themselves mainly by metabolic processes, and ectotherms, which depend upon external heat from the environment. Reptiles are ectothermal: they regulate their temperatures largely by their behavior. When presented their bodies reach the preferred temperature. From their behavior, it appears that the optimal temperature for metabolism must be surprisingly close to the critical upper temperature at which the animals seek shade.

After basking, land and desert tortoises retreat into cool burrows. Not infrequently they emerge again in the evening and continue to bask until the sun begins to set. In general, they lead a leisurely existence, getting up late and retiring early. At the time of midday retreat to the burrow, the temperature on the top shell of the American desert tortoise may be as much as fifty degrees above the deep body temperature. Both heating and cooling rates are affected by thermal gradients between the core of the animal and the temperature of the environment.

Some years ago I worked with nuclear physicist David Butt on Mediterranean spur-thighed tortoises. These tortoises live on the fringe of the Sahara where they estivate during the hottest part of summer and hibernate in winter, becoming active only in the spring and fall. When we measured metabolism and evaporation at different air temperatures, we learned that up to about 75° F the metabolic heat gained and evaporative heat lost were about equal. At higher temperatures, however, evaporative heat loss could not keep pace with metabolic heat production. These experiments led us to speculate that with the advent of seasonal climates 60 million years ago, hot summers rather than cold winters might have had something to do with the demise of dinosaurs. Our calculations showed that large size would have been a useful strategy for reptiles in a stable, moderately warm climate, but higher temperatures were likely to cause severe thermal stress.

During our work on temperature physiology, one of the tortoises ate the cobalt thiocyanate paper used to monitor humidity, defecated over the temperature sensors, and blocked the entry port for air, so that it nearly suffocated. "We certainly have technical problems in physics research," my partner from the "hard sciences" commented, "but never have I experienced anything like this!"

TWELVE MEN AND A TURTLE
Lenape folktale

When bad men and turtles meet, this Lenape story suggests, put your money on the chelonians.

There was once a gang of twelve men who were always killing and robbing people. One day these men set off to hunt for victims. They traveled a long way, over many days and nights, but they could never find any other people.

As they traveled, they found a huge turtle whose back was furrowed with deep paths. They climbed these until they reached the turtle's back. They decided they could use the turtle as a vehicle and save having to walk, and so they traveled like this for several days. When they arrived at the Big Water the turtle plunged in. The twelve men tried to get off, but all but one of them were too slow, and they disappeared under the water.

The one who escaped went to a Shawnee camp and begged the medicine man to help. He sang a song that he swore would make the men return.

The medicine man and some other Shawnee sat alongside the Big Water and sang. They heard a roar, and then a giant crayfish appeared. The medicine man said, "No, we want the turtle, not you." Then a big snake appeared, and the medicine man said the same thing.

Eventually the turtle appeared. The men were still on his back, and they were still alive.

The turtle came right up to the medicine man, who said, "Give him tobacco. Whenever you want anything from an animal, you should give it tobacco."

The medicine man tied a bundle of tobacco to the turtle's neck. When he did, the eleven men turned and looked around, as if they had just been awakened from a dream. They climbed down from the turtle's back and went up to the medicine man.

"We have been all over the world," they said. "Under the Big Water lies a world like ours, but it has no sunlight. It is full of people and full of animals."

After that, the men did not rob and kill, for they supposed that they were being punished for their crimes by having to ride on the turtle's back into the other world. They went home and behaved themselves. The Lenape still have the Shawnee medicine, in case that turtle comes back.

SEA TURTLES
Aristotle

In his Historia Animalia, *Aristotle attempts to classify the kinds of turtles known to the ancients.*

Animals then have been categorized into terrestrial and aquatic in three ways, according to their assumption of air or of water, the temperament of their bodies, or the character of their food; and the mode of life of an animal corresponds to the category in which it is found. That is to say, in some cases the animal depends for its terrestrial or aquatic nature on temperament and diet combined, as well as on its method of respiration; and sometimes on temperament and habits alone.

Of testaceans, some, that are incapable of motion, subsist on fresh water, for, as the sea water dissolves into its constituents, the fresh water from its greater thinness percolates through the grosser parts; in fact, they live on fresh water just as they were originally engendered from the same. Now that fresh water is contained in the sea and can be strained off from it can be proved in a thoroughly practical way. Take a thin vessel of molded wax, attach a cord to it, and let it down quite empty into the sea: in twenty-four hours it will be found to contain a quantity of water, and the water will be fresh and drinkable.

Sea anemones feed on such small fishes as come in their way. The mouth of this creature is in the middle of its body; and this fact may be clearly observed in the case of the larger varieties. Like the oyster it has a duct for the outlet of the residuum; and this duct is at the top of the animal. In other words, the sea-anemone corresponds to the inner fleshy part of the oyster, and the stone to which the one creature clings corresponds to the shell which encases the other.

The limpet detaches itself from the rock and goes about in quest of food. Of shellfish that are mobile, some are carnivorous and live on little fishes, as for instance, the purple murex—and there can be no doubt that the purple murex is carnivorous, as it is caught by a bait of fish; others are carnivorous, but feed also on marine vegetation.

The sea-turtles feed on shellfish. Their mouths are extraordinarily hard; whatever object it seizes, stone or other, it crunches into bits, but when it leaves the water for dry land it browses on grass. These creatures suffer greatly, and often die when they lie on the surface of the water exposed to a scorching sun; for, once they have risen to the surface, they find it difficult to sink again.

translated by Gregory McNamee

ALBANIAN TORTOISES
Edith Durham

In 1900, Edith Durham, a proper late Victorian lady, left England to seek the sun on her doctor's orders. She found it in Albania, little visited then as now. She also found a number of traditions that seemed charming to her, such as this one, which she recorded in her 1909 memoir **High Albania.**

A proverb says: "Each disease has its herb."

A popular dressing for cuts and wounds is the common St. John's Wort (*Hypericum perforate*) well pounded and put into a bottle of olive oil. This must be placed in the sun for several days, and is then fit for use. It has such a reputation for healing that I think it must have some antiseptic property.

A remedy for jaundice, a common complaint in the mountains, is: catch a little fish, put it in a basin of water and stare at it steadily as it swims round. After a few days the yellow goes out of your eyes into the fish, and you are cured.

A wondrous plant is that which breaks stone and iron. Should a hobbled horse, out grazing, touch it with the hobble the iron flies asunder. Valuable horses have often thus been lost. None knows where the plant grows but the tortoise.

When you find, as is not infrequent, some tortoise's eggs, you must build a little wall round them of stones.

Then hide and await the mother tortoise. She will be very angry and strive to butt down the wall with her head, lest her children should hatch inside it and be starved. Failing to butt it down she will go and fetch a leaf of the plant, touch the wall with it, and at once down goes the wall!

You can then take the leaf from her, and use it for burglary and other household purposes. Where she finds it none knows, and she will not fetch it if followed.

Tortoises swarm in Albania—oddly fascinating beasts that bask in the sun and peer at you with little beady eyes, or walk along serenely, craning their wrinkled necks and browsing with deliberate bites off the leaves they fancy; sad things are they in a sprouting maize or bean field. It is not surprising that their grotesque form has inspired a folktale: How the Tortoise Got its Shell.

When Christ was crucified all the beasts hastened to condole with the Virgin Mary. The poor little tortoise was deeply grieved, and did not know how to show his grief; so, on the way, he bit off a large leaf and covered himself up. When the Virgin saw him coming along with only his little head sticking out, he looked so funny that she could not help laughing aloud in spite of the painful circumstances. And the tortoise has been covered up ever since.

AN IRRESISTIBLE NECESSITY FOR TURTLES

Henry David Thoreau

The title says it all: humans who know turtles' ways find turtles of all kinds utterly necessary in the world, a point that Henry David Thoreau ruminated on at length in his journals.

> *Nature does not forget beauty of outline*
> *even in a mud turtle's shell.*

How much lies quietly buried in the ground that we wot not of! We unconsciously step over the eggs of snapping turtles slowly hatching the summer through. Not only was the surface perfectly dry and trackless there, but blackberry vines had run over the spot where these eggs were buried and weeds had sprung up above. If Iliads are not composed in our day, snapping turtles are hatched and arrive at maturity. It already thrusts forth its tremendous head,—for the first time in this sphere,—and slowly moves from side to side,—opening its small glistening eyes for the first time to the light,—expressive of dull rage, as if it had endured the trials of this world for a century. When I behold this monster thus steadily advancing toward maturity, all nature abetting, I am convinced there must be an irresistible necessity for mud turtles. With what tenacity Nature sticks to her idea! These eggs, not warm to the touch, buried in the ground, so slow to hatch, are like the seeds of vegetable life.

~

Black Willows on the Assabet
They are none of them upright, but in this case, close under a higher wood of maples and swamp white oak, slant over the stream, and, taken separately or viewed from the land side, are very imperfect trees. If you stand at their base and look upward or outward, you see a great proportion of naked trunk but thinly invested with foliage even at the summit, and they are among the most unsightly trees. The lower branches slant downward from the main divisions so as commonly to rest on the water....

The *Sternothaerus odoratus* knows them well, for it climbs highest up their stems, three or four feet or more nowadays, sometimes seven or eight along the slanting branches, and is frequently caught and hung by the neck in its forks. They do not so much jump as tumble off when disturbed by a passer. The small black mud tortoise, with its muddy shell, eyes you motionless from its resting-place in a fork of the black willow. They will climb four feet up a stem not more than two inches in diameter, and yet undo all their work in an instant by tumbling off when your boat goes by. The trunk is covered with coarse, long, and thick upraised scales. It is this turtle's castle and path to heaven. He is on the upward road along the stem of the willow, and by its dark stem it is partially concealed. Yes, the musquash and the mud tortoise and the bittern know it well....

How long will it be after we have passed before the mud tortoise has climbed to its perch again?

~

There was no boat on Little Quitticus; so we could not explore it. Set out to walk round it, but, the water being high,—higher than anciently even, on account of dams,—we had to go round a swamp at the south end, about Joe's Rocks, and R. gave it up. I went to Long Pond and waited for him. Saw a strange turtle, much like a small snapping turtle or very large *Sternothaerus odoratus*, crawling slowly along the bottom next to shore. Poked it ashore with a stick. It had a peculiarly square snout, two hinges to the sternum and both parts movable. Was very sluggish; would not snap nor bite. Looked old, being mossy above on the edge, and the scales greenish and eaten beneath. The flesh slate-colored.

I saw that it was new and wished to bring it away, but had no paper to wrap it in. So I peeled a white birch, getting a piece of bark about ten inches long. I noticed that the birch sap was flowing. This bark at once curled back so as to present its yellow side outward. I rolled it about the turtle and folded the ends back and tied it round with a strip of birch bark, making a very nice and airy box for the creature, which would not be injured by moisture, far better than any paper, and so I brought it home to Concord at last. As my coat hung in R.'s shanty, over a barrel of paper, the morning that I came away the turtle made a little noise, scratching the birch bark in my pocket. R. observed,

"There is a mouse in that barrel. What would you do about it?" "Oh, let him alone," said I, "he'll get out directly." "They often get among my papers," he added. "I guess I'd better set the barrel outdoors." I did not explain, and perhaps he experimented on the barrel after my departure.

∽

Coming across the level pasture west of E. Hubbard's swamp, towards Emerson's, I find a young *Emys insculpta*, apparently going to lay, though she had not dug a hole. It was four and a quarter inches long by three and a half wide, and altogether the handsomest turtle of this species, if not of any, that I have ever seen. It was quite fresh and perfect, without wound or imperfection; its claws quite sharp and slender, and the annual striae so distinct on all the scales above and below that I could count them with ease. It was nine years old, though it would be like an infant among turtles, the successive striae being perfectly parallel at equal distances apart. The sternum, with a large black spot on the rear angle of each scale and elsewhere a rich brown color, even reminded me of the turtle shell of commerce. While its upper shell was of a uniform wholesome brown, very prettily marked indeed, not only by the outlines of the scales, but more distinctly by the lines of prominence raying out from the starting-point of each scale, perfectly preserved in each year's growth, a most elaborate coat of mail, worthy the lifelong labor of some reptilian Vulcan. This must have been a belle among the *E. insculpta*. Nevertheless I did discover that all the claws but one of one hind foot were gone! Had not a bird pecked them off? So liable are they to injury in their long lives. Then they are so well-behaved; can be taken up and brought home in your pocket, and make no unseemly efforts to escape.

adapted from The Journals

TORTUGA

Luis Alberto Urrea

*Returning to the site of Thoreau's most famous book, Luis Urrea
finds much changed—but much the same.*

Walden Pond. Today.

To travelers who come from afar, seeking Henry Thoreau's wilderness in this famous place, Walden must be a bit
of a shock. In my part of the world, for example, "pond"
always meant a small muddy watering hole full of craw-
dads: this thing's a lake, if it's anything. Nobody from the
Southwest would mistake it for a pond.

I first saw it in October. I had come from San Diego
and Tijuana into the astonishment of New England's fall. I
have ever since equated Walden with the fall, my favorite
season, when the sun—from its southern migration—must
slant its light sideways onto the water. The colors are an
affront. And the sunlight picks each leaf out, ignites it as if
it were on fire, and burns it as it tumbles to the ground.

The surface of the pond was drifting with flame: flotil-
las of orange, red, yellow, almost purple leaves bobbed and
collected along the shore. The pond was in flood, riding
high over its banks, and you could stand on wooden
benches surrounded by leafy water.

Utterly unfazed by any of this, a row of old white men
stood fishing. (Thoreau: "Time is but the stream I go a-fish-
ing in.") Among these old men was an arthritic dalmatian

named Jason. He walked at an angle, snorting, stiff, tail inscribing oblong loops in the air.

"Hork," he said, through a curled lip.

I had taken the train from Somerville, half excited and half afraid. And when I'd gotten to Concord, I set out in the wrong direction, walking into the woods and gawking at pumpkins in the kinds of fields I had only seen on greeting cards. A local in a pickup turned me around, and a few miles of leisurely hiking later, I found Walden.

That coat of floating leaves! Flat and dense as scales: Walden looked like a huge aquatic snake had shed its skin, rubbing against the benches, the shore-trees, the unmoving legs of the old fishermen.

⁓

In the summer, Walden has many swimmers—pale city folks from Boston and Cambridge: housewives with infants, rock bands, secretaries taking a mental health day, retirees. Canoes. Rubber rafts. Frisbees. Running along the edge of the woods above Thoreau's cabin site is a four-lane highway. There is a run-down trailer park at Walden; behind this, a garbage dump. You can park your car in the state lot for $3.00. Along the western shore of the pond, the Concord-to-Boston commuter train runs, carrying daily loads of purple-haired teenagers suffering through Walden in their English classes and wondering what's the big deal. But why complain? Like Thoreau, we take transcendence where we can find it.

⁓

Summer's relentless traffic jam closes the parking lot at about noon. This forces the cars out on the street, which fills along each edge by 12:15. The flow then creeps across the highway and down the country road, toward Concord (pronounced, locally, as "Conquered"). If you are early enough to get a coveted spot in the $3 lot, you can see an exact replica of Thoreau's cabin. I always imagined a rustic beauty, some sort of nineteenth century solar A-frame, perhaps, with decks and a hot-tub. The cabin, too, can come as a shock.

The whole thing, including cot, fireplace, table, austere wooden chair, is about the same size as the bedroom in a small urban apartment. Thoreau's modesty here is echoed at his grave. If you go to Author's Ridge in Sleepy Hollow Cemetery, you'll find him buried near Emerson, the Alcotts, and Hawthorne. You can imagine their conversations on late Halloween nights. Thoreau has a tiny white stone. With great poignancy, its sole message is: Henry.

$\sim$

The actual cabin site is close to shore. You have to walk to it. It is clearly pointed out by signs at water's edge that read:

CABIN SITE

The main trail around Walden takes you to Thoreau's yard, whether you want to go there or not. All you do is turn right at the public toilet and keep going. You'll come to a small inlet and a black bog. Frogs leap away from you, crying, "Yikes!" The trail jerks a hard left at the bog, and there you are.

You will find a small stone floor, a rustic sign. That's about it.

People have built a memorial cairn of stones in honor of Henry. It was begun by the Alcotts. If you think about it, you can actually hear the clack of that first flat stone falling, and a mumbled word of sorrow and honor on the chill air. Visitors continue to bring Henry rocks from all over the world—stones from the Himalayas mix with pebbles from the Walden bath house. I drop my bit of crumbling granite and am disappointed by the size of the pile. This is Thoreau, after all; surely, the cairn should be a silo by now, a tower.

~

When I float in the inlet near the cabin, I like to imagine him up there, pondering the pond from the shore. He must have come right here, to my own favorite spot below the cabin, every evening. I imagine his old ghost wavering amid the trees; I can just about see his thoughts rising like pipe smoke. And here, in the overcrowded inlet of water nearest the highway, I stumbled across a piece of the wild past, true and hard and untamed.

~

Walden has its share of living beings, aside from lifeguards and state police on horseback. Nature, including us, attempts to carry on, undaunted. Squirrels and truck-loads of insects and amphibians live here; fish are abundant—especially the gregarious little sunfish. They follow your feet as you walk in the shallows, seemingly amazed and excited by your feet. You reach out with your toe and tap one of them on the nose: it will back up, startled, shake it off, and rush back for a closer look. On any day, you can look into the water and see yourself surrounded by five or six fish, arrayed in spokes, hypnotized by the sight of your feet.

One day, I was swimming across the inlet, parting the colorful scum of cocoa-butter and sun block that swirls at the surface. Making headway through the mysterious spurts of hot water that well up through the chill water for no clear reason (passing swimmers look at each other suspiciously). Generally doing my best to ignore the various louts, gawkers, rangers, bikinis, radios, lawn chairs, and squealing styrofoam doodads.

Something, however, rose.

It was out in the middle, at a point equally distant from each edge of the water. It was a rock. No it wasn't, rocks can't float. It was a log. It was a rotting human foot.

I swam to about an arm-and-a-half's length away and shook the water from my eyes. It was a turtle. A big turtle. It turned its head and regarded me with a cool gaze. Up close, its blunt face looked like the front of a Santa Fe locomotive (F-7 Freight Diesel).

A snapping turtle. Too young, no doubt, to have known Henry. But I bet its mother knew him.

The old snapper's shell could be seen as a congealed oval of darkness hanging just beneath the surface. Legs dangling loose. I moved. His head disappeared with a plip! then slowly came back up. We were suspended there, in a bubble of silence. (Actually, he was suspended; I was paddling furiously.)

Chelydra serpentina is a frightening animal. At certain times of the year, huge females wander about the land, looking for egg-laying sites and terrorizing the community. Their jaws are powerful, and they are not shy about threatening to bite. Local folklore has it that they can bite through broomsticks with a single chomp; local boys habitually bother them with sticks, hoping for a snap. I once had a baby snapper the size of a fifty-cent piece clamp himself to my thumb and hang there with the fiercest look in his eye. He seemed to be daring me to get his jaws unlatched.

When the Walden turtle dipped its head, my first thought was of toes being snipped away, thick gouges of thigh being torn loose.

His shell seemed to be about two feet long, but it was hard to tell. His mean hooked mouth. His piercing metal eye. The air cut a blue cave around us.

Then, he sank. No fanfare, no apparent effort at all: Walden's murk grayed him and made him seem, as he sank, as though he were being shaved thinner and thinner, until only a clear wafer of shell was left. The wafer turned to glass. The turtle was gone.

A POOL OF TURTLES

Ibn Sara

Ibn Sara, a Moorish soldier and poet, lived in Santarén, a town in Andalusia, until his death in 1123. There he kept a freshwater pond full of turtles, which he celebrates in this verse.

Thick eyelashes
and a thick pupil
among the flowers
of this secluded pool
this beautiful pool

Full of turtles
they leap, submerge
and rise
clothed in mossy green
and fight
for the best place at the water's edge
until winter
when they sink

They stay hidden below
but in the summer
they emerge and scoot
and look around them
just like Christian soldiers
bearing shields

translated by Gregory McNamee

PACK TURTLES
Arizona folklore

This bit of local legend concerning Xerobates agassizii *comes from the* Wickenburg News-Herald *of December 11, 1903.*

Harrisburg was the scene of quite a sensation Sunday and if what was seen here then is any indication of what may be done, the problem of desert travel and transportation where water is scarce will soon be settled. Frank Midlon, who has been prospecting in the Harqua Hala and Harcuvar Mountains for the past two years, came here Saturday afternoon after provisions, as he is in the habit of doing every three months. Instead of bringing his five pack burros as usual, Mr. Midlon came sauntering into town leading a monster terrapin, the same dry land turtle as you have around Wickenburg, only much larger.

According to Mr. Midlon, the terrapin, which he calls Jumbo, weighs about four hundred and fifty pounds and can pack from twelve hundred to fifteen hundred pounds, according to the roughness of the country. Three of Mr. Midlon's burros died last winter on account of lack of feed and water near his camp and the other two wandered off, leaving him "up against it," as he had to pack his camp water eight miles to where he is working in the Harcuvar Mountains. Not wishing to make the long trip here after new burros, he finally decided to try a terrapin, and after using him, he says he would not trade Jumbo for a dozen burros. Two holes have been bored in the edge of the upper shell on each side, enabling a pack to be securely tied on. After spending Sunday morning packing some of the boys around town, just to show what Jumbo could do, Mr. Midlon left that afternoon for the Socorro mine to have Jumbo shod by blacksmith Ed Towner.

He returned yesterday afternoon, bearing evidence of Towner's skill in the shape of four sole leather shoes, studded with bob nails. Mr. Midlon loaded up with his usual supply of grub, amounting to over seven hundred pounds and after securing it tightly with the ordinary diamond hitch, started back to camp yesterday afternoon, Jumbo apparently not noticing the load of seven hundred pounds any more than the empty pack saddle.

The distance to Mr. Midlon's camp is about thirty-five miles and he says he can make the trip loaded in about five days easy traveling. If the supply of terrapins lasts, there will be no further use for burros in this section, as the terrapins can go without water for two months or more without suffering any inconvenience, and a little hay or greasewood once a month is an ample supply of food. Mr. Midlon said he had no trouble at all in breaking Jumbo and that when he camps at night he simply ties both legs on one side together, so that if he tries to get away he walks around in a circle and makes no progress.

TURTLE SONGS
Traditional Japanese folksongs

Japanese poetry is full of animals. Cuckoos, frogs, and dragonflies make many appearances there, but turtles are relatively uncommon. These poems are more exceptions to the rule.

In the ocean
  the ageless turtle plays.
On its back
  stand the three holy mountains,
    Horai, Hojo, Eishu.

The years of these mountains
  and of the turtle bearing them,
   added all together,
  I would wish for you.
All of that, I'd give to you.

~

From high,
the moon shines on Mount Shumi.
It shines upon the water of the Lotus Pond.

There's a turtle at the waterside,
where the Seven Gems gleam.

It's playing there
as eternity glides by.

~

What wretched creatures
we who fish with cormorants are!

I have killed the turtles
which were meant to live a thousand years,
and bound my birds' throats.

I may go on living in this way
in this world
—but how will I live through the next?

translated by Yasuhiko Moriguchi and David Jenkins

PROVERBS AND SAYINGS

Turtles play a role in the proverbs of many cultures—and not only on account of their deliberate pace.

Long legs mean nothing to a turtle.

Japanese

The tortoise does not have milk to give, but it knows how to care for its child.

Ashanti

A turtle lays a thousand eggs without anyone's knowing it; a hen lays one egg and the whole town hears.

Malay

A grazing tortoise is no good to eat, for it eats earth all winter long.

Albanian

A piece of wood always floats near a blind tortoise just when it is in need of help.

Japanese

Behold the turtle: he makes progress only when he sticks his neck out.

American

When a tortoise burns himself he keeps his pain to himself.

Chinese

Just because he is round does not mean that the snapping turtle should be compared to the moon.

Japanese

Even a tortoise can climb a fallen tree.

Malay

As the saying goes: the turtle was sent for yeast at Christmas—and came back at Easter.

Polish

TRICKSTER

Tukano (South American Indian) myth

The spirit identified as Coyote in North America takes a different form in the South.

The turtle is a trickster. He was in the forest and saw some monkeys in an ëhná palm. The turtle called: "Cousin, what are you doing there?" He asked them to throw him some fruit. The monkeys said: "Cousin, are you a woman that you can't climb up?" "Certainly not," said the turtle; "I am coming up." The monkeys helped her. The turtle ate, and after a while the monkeys left. Then the turtle stayed clinging to the branches, up there, for a year. He was on his last fruit. He could not get down. The birds made fun of him, and the toucan, the paca, and all the birds too. He could not get down. Then a jaguar came by. He saw some turtle excrement below and looked up. "What is this old girl doing up there?" the jaguar said. The turtle answered: "You don't know how to climb up here." The jaguar asked for some fruit, and the turtle threw it down to him. He liked it and asked for more. Then the turtle said: "Jaguar, man; stand still just below me, with your eyes closed." The turtle let herself fall on top of the jaguar and nothing happened to her, but the jaguar died because the turtle fell right between his eyebrows. But the turtle was hungry; she waited until the jaguar was rotten. After three days she called her family together, and they ate the jaguar. Then she pulled a bone out of its leg. She made a flute out of it and played it: "This is the bone of my cousin the jaguar who is a big coward!" Then the other jaguars took notice. War broke out between the jaguars and the turtles. Quite often one finds a turtle shell in the forest, with toothmarks of some jaguar. The jaguars asked: "What is it the turtle sings?" The turtle played and sang, and then she withdrew into her shell.

The turtle met the fox. There was a hole in the ground, and the turtle hid in it. The fox stayed around waiting. The turtle likes to eat pineapple, and the fox said: "I bet that you can't stay in this hole until the pineapples ripen." They bet this, and the fox stopped up the hole. A week went by. "What's up?" said the fox. "Are you still alive?" Six months went by until the pineapple ripened. They made another bet. "Now wait until I eat the pineapple," the turtle said. Now the fox went into the hole, and the turtle stopped it up. After three days he died of hunger. The turtle invited her family, and they ate the fox. She removed a bone and made a flute out of it and played it: "This is the bone of my cousin the fox who is a big coward!" Already the turtle had two enemies: the jaguar and the fox.

Then the turtle met the deer. "Cousin, let's bet to see who can run faster!" They went to the forest, which was very dense, some three or four kilometers. They made trails, one for the turtle and another for the deer. But the turtle placed fifty relatives every ten or fifteen steps. The deer ran, and the agreement was that he who was ahead should call from the front. The deer called: "Cousin turtle!" The turtle would answer from the front. This went on until the deer died. When he became rotten, the turtle ate him and made a flute and sang: "This is the bone of my cousin the deer who is a big coward!" Now there were three enemies.

Then he met the tapir. When he wanted to bet with him, the tapir kicked him and left him sprawling on his back in the mud. Some years went by. Finally a guinea pig came. "Please, help me!" the turtle said. The guinea pig dug and set him free. The turtle was furious at the tapir. The tapir, when he walks through the forest, leaves a lot of excrement. The turtle went to find it. From the excrement, plants grow because the tapir eats a lot of seeds. First the turtle went along finding dry excrement. He followed it asking along the way. Finally, the turtle found fresh excrement, about six months old. He measured the size of the plants that grew from the seeds in the excrement. Thus, he knew how far away the tapir was. Then he found warm excrement. He found the tapir sleeping. He walked around it until he saw his testicles. Then he decided to bite them. The tapir woke up, but the turtle kept hold of his testicles and killed the tapir. This is why the payés [hunters] invoke the turtle, for his physical cunning against the evil beasts. The turtle is almost indestructible. They invoke him like this: "Big turtle, little turtle; black-colored turtle, red-colored turtle; great turtle of the river; your teeth, your shell; under your protection I defend myself." This is how they invoke the turtle.

retold by Gerardo Reichel-Dolmatoff

MAKING THE SIGN
OF THE TORTOISE
W. P. Clark

If you wished to communicate on the High Plains of the nineteenth century and spoke no Native American languages, you could still make yourself understood—but only if you had mastered a complex sign language. Linguist W. P. Clark here describes how to indicate "turtle."

Hold right hand, back up, in front of and lower than right shoulder, hand near body, hand nearly closed, but back of fingers from knuckles to second joints nearly on line with back of hand; move the hand horizontally to front, at same time, by wrist action; twist the hand to right and left.

Some Indians make sign for water, shape of the animal, and move the hands to imitate motion of its feet.

PARTRIDGE AND TURTLE
Mbundu folktale

In the folklore of the Mbundu of Angola, turtles are crafty, and not to be trusted.

I will tell of Partridge who had a discussion with Turtle.

Partridge said: "Thou, friend Turtle, never canst run away. When the fire is coming into the land, thou art always burnt." Turtle said: "I cannot be burnt. Thou art burnt, thou, Partridge." Partridge said: "I have my wings; I fly. Thou canst not fly, canst not run; thou shalt burn just here, in this very same place." They were silent.

They spent days; the dry season came. The fires begin over the country. The bush, where are Turtle and Partridge, it is set on fire. The fire approaches where Turtle is; Turtle gets into an anthill. It comes where Partridge is; Partridge runs; it will not do. The fire comes nearer him; he begins to fly from the fire. The fire catches him; he is burnt.

The fire came to an end in our country in that season. The hunters, who had come to the fire-hunt, had scattered. Turtle comes out of the anthill; he looks on the ground; Partridge is burnt! He says: "What! comrade Partridge, I had with him that discussion, he saying 'thou shalt be burnt;' but he himself was burnt."

Turtle took him by the leg; he took off from him a spur. He begins to play with the spur of Partridge, saying:

Little horn of Partridge,
Partridge is dead,
The little horn is left.

Partridge had a discussion with Turtle; Partridge was burnt;
Turtle escaped.

GALÁPAGOS TORTOISES
Charles Darwin

The turtles of the Galápagos Islands, off the west coast of Ecuador, can grow to five feet long and weigh in at 450 pounds. They are also reputed to live to the ripe old age of two hundred years, although, as with other turtles, that is the exception and not the rule. Here the noted biologist Charles Darwin describes them at first hand.

We will now turn to the order of reptiles, which gives the most striking character to the zoology of these islands. The species are not numerous, but the numbers of individuals of each species are extraordinarily great. There is one small lizard belonging to a South American genus, and two species (and probably more) of the Amblythynchus—a genus confined to the Galápagos Islands. There is one snake which is numerous; it is identical, as I am informed by M. Bibron, with the Psammophis Temminckii from Chile. Of sea-turtle I believe there is more than one species; and of tortoises there are, as we shall presently show, two or three species or races....

I will first describe the habits of the tortoise (Testudo nigra, formerly called Indica), which has been so frequently alluded to. These animals are found, I believe, on all the islands of the Archipelago; certainly on the greater number. They frequent in preference the high damp parts, but they likewise live in the lower and arid districts. I have already shown, from the numbers which have been caught in a single day, how very numerous they must be. Some grow to an immense size: Mr. Lawson, an Englishman, and vice-governor of the colony, told us that he had seen several so large, that it required six or eight men to lift them from the ground; and that some had afforded as much as two hundred pounds of meat. The old males are the largest, the females rarely growing to so great a size: the male can readily be distinguished from the female by the greater length of its tail. The tortoises which live on those islands where there is no water, or in the lower and arid parts of the others, feed chiefly on the succulent cactus. Those which frequent the higher and damp regions, eat the leaves of various trees, a kind of berry (called guayavita) which is acid and austere, and likewise a pale green filamentous lichen (*Usnea plicata*), that hangs in tresses from the boughs of the trees.

The tortoise is very fond of water, drinking large quantities, and wallowing in the mud. The larger islands alone possess springs, and these are always situated towards the central parts, and at a considerable height. The tortoises, therefore, which frequent the lower districts, when thirsty, are obliged to travel from a long distance. Hence broad and well-beaten paths branch off in every direction from the wells down to the sea-coast; and the Spaniards by following them up, first discovered the watering-places. When I landed at Chatham Island, I could not imagine what animal travelled so methodically along well-chosen tracks. Near the springs it was a curious spectacle to behold many of these huge creatures, one set eagerly travelling onwards with outstretched necks, and another set returning, after having drunk their fill. When the tortoise arrives at the spring, quite regardless of any spectator, he buries his head in the water above his eyes, and greedily swallows great mouthfuls, at the rate of about ten in a minute. The inhabitants say each animal stays three or four days in the neighbourhood of the water, and then returns to the lower country; but they differed respecting the frequency of these visits. The animal probably regulates them according to the nature of the food on which it has lived. It is, however, certain, that tortoises can subsist even on those islands, where there is no other water than what falls during a few rainy days in the year.

I believe it is well ascertained, that the bladder of the frog acts as a reservoir for the moisture necessary to its existence: such seems to be the case with the tortoise. For some time after a visit to the springs, their urinary bladders are distended with fluid, which is said gradually to decrease in volume, and to become less pure. The inhabitants, when walking in the lower district, and overcome with thirst, often take advantage of this circumstance, and drink the contents of the bladder if full: in one I saw killed, the fluid was quite limpid, and had only a very slightly bitter taste. The inhabitants, however, always first drink the water in the pericardium, which is described as being best.

The tortoises, when purposely moving towards any point, travel by night and day, and arrive at their journey's end much sooner than would be expected. The inhabitants, from observing marked individuals, consider that they travel a distance of about eight miles in two or three days. One large tortoise, which I watched, walked at the rate of sixty yards in ten minutes, that is 360 yards in the hour, or four miles a day,—allowing a little time for it to eat on the road. During the breeding season, when the male and female are together, the male utters a hoarse roar or bellowing, which, it is said, can be heard at the distance of more than a hundred yards. The female never uses her voice, and the male only at these times; so that when the people hear this noise, they know that the two are together. They were at this time (October) laying their eggs. The female, where the soil is sandy, deposits them together, and covers them up with sand; but where the ground is rocky she drops them indiscriminately in any hole: Mr. Bynoe found seven placed in a fissure. The egg is white and spherical; one which I measured was seven inches and three-eighths in circumference, and therefore larger than a hen's egg. The young tortoises, as soon as they are hatched, fall a prey in great numbers to the carrion-feeding buzzard. The old ones seem generally to die from accidents, as from falling down precipices: at least, several of the inhabitants told me, that they had never found one dead without some evident cause.

The inhabitants believe that these animals are absolutely deaf; certainly they do not overhear a person walking close behind them. I was always amused when overtaking one of these great monsters, as it was quietly pacing along, to see how suddenly, the instant I passed, it would draw in its head and legs, and uttering a deep hiss fall to the ground with a heavy sound, as if struck dead. I frequently got on their backs, and then giving a few raps on the hinder part of their sheds, they would rise up and walk away;—but I found it very difficult to keep my balance. The flesh of this animal is largely employed, both fresh and salted; and a beautifully clear oil is prepared from the fat. When a tortoise is caught, the man makes a slit in the skin near its tail, so as to see inside its body, whether the fat under the dorsal plate is thick. If it is not, the animal is liberated; and it is said to recover soon from this strange operation. In order to secure the tortoises, it is not sufficient to turn them like turtle, for they are often able to get on their legs again.

There can be little doubt that this tortoise is an aboriginal inhabitant of the Galapagos; for it is found on all, or nearly all, the islands, even on some of the smaller ones where there is no water; had it been an imported species, this would hardly have been the case in a group which has been so little frequented. Moreover, the old Bucaniers found this tortoise in greater numbers even than at present: Wood and Rogers also, in 1708, say that it is the opinion of the Spaniards, that it is found nowhere else in this quarter of the world. It is now widely distributed; but it may be questioned whether it is in any other place an aboriginal. The bones of a tortoise at Mauritius, associated with those of the extinct Dodo, have generally been considered as belonging to this tortoise: if this had been so, undoubtedly it must have been there indigenous; but M. Bibron informs me that he believes that it was distinct, as the species now living there certainly is.

THE MAGICAL TORTOISE
Assamese folktale

A turtle brings relief to a suffering family.

Once there was a rich farmer who had two wives. The younger wife, who was his favorite, had a son, Teja, and a daughter, Teji. The older wife had a daughter, but no son.

Jealous, she went with the younger wife to the farmer's pond to bathe. She pushed the younger wife below the surface and shouted, "Change into a tortoise and remain as one!" The younger wife immediately became a big tortoise.

The next day Teja and Teji went to the pond to water the farmer's cattle. The older wife had refused to feed them, and they were hungry. The tortoise rose up from the bottom and cried, "Children, it's me, your mother! I am no longer here to feed you!" And then she vomited on a banana leaf and invited them to eat.

They did, and their hunger was gone. Every day they returned, and every day their mother vomited up a little food for them, more than enough to keep them alive.

The older wife took notice that her rival's children, who by all rights should have starved to death, looked well-fed. Her own daughter, whom she lavished with butter and rice and vegetables, did not look so healthy. So the older wife sent that daughter out to follow Teja and Teji and see where they were getting their food.

The daughter followed them and saw them eating what the tortoise had given them. They saw her, though, and called her over. "You may have a share of our food if you don't tell your mother about it," Teja and Teji whispered. The daughter assented, and ate.

When her daughter returned, the older wife saw that she seemed very well-fed. The daughter denied having eaten anything outside her mother's kitchen, but when her mother began to beat her, she confessed.

That night the older wife put some broken crockery under her mattress. Whenever she tossed and turned, the crockery shattered some more. The rich farmer, who believed that his younger wife had deserted him, lay alongside her in her bed. He turned to her and said, "What's the matter? What's all that noise?"

The older wife said, "Ah, my bones are getting creaky. What I need is some turtle flesh and turtle oil to ease my pains. Go kill that tortoise out in your pond and help me get better."

Teja and Teji overheard all this, and they ran to the pond to tell their mother what was about to happen. She said, "Children, only you can catch me, and that will gain you favor with your father. When he serves me up, don't eat my flesh. Bury it out beside this pond, and soon a tree of gold and silver will grow where I lie."

So they caught their mother, and gave her to the farmer, who made her into a fine curry. Teja and Teji did not eat the flesh, but buried it.

Their mother's flesh grew up into a tree full of gold and silver, and Teja and Teji became rich, with enough money to leave that sorrowful farm and their evil stepmother behind.

TURTLE
José Juan Tablada

Octavio Paz credits his fellow Mexican poet José Juan Tablada
with introducing Japanese poetic forms into the Spanish language.
Certainly this small poem to a turtle has a haiku-like feel.

Although he never changes houses,
the turtle totters along like a moving van
down the road

translated by Gregory McNamee

FLORIDA TORTOISES
William Bartram

Field observations, the stuff of objective science, give way to delight in the journals of William Bartram, the early-nineteenth-century explorer of the American South.

Crossing another large deep creek of St. Juan's, the country is a vast level plain, and the soil good for the distance of four or five miles, though light and sandy, producing a forest of stately pines and laurels, with some others; and a vast profusion of herbage, such as rudbeckia, helianthus, silphium, polymnia, ruellia, verbena, rhexea, convolvulus, sophora, glycine, vitia, clitorea, ipomea, urtica, salvia graveolens, viola, and many more. How cheerful and social is the rural converse of the various tribes of tree frogs, whilst they look to heaven for prolific showers! How harmonious the shrill tuneful songs of the wood thrush, and the soothing love lays of the amorous cuckoo, seated in the cool leafy branches of the stately magnolias and shadowy elms, maples and liquidambar, together with gigantic fagus sylvatica, which shade and perfume these sequestered groves! How unexpected and enchanting the enjoyment, after traversing a burning sandy desert!

Now, again, we behold the open pine forests, and ascend the sandy hills, which continue for some miles, then gently descend again, when a level expansive savanna plain presents itself to view, which, after entering, and proceeding on, becomes wet and covered by a fine short grass, with extensive parterres of the dwarf creeping palmetto, its stipes sharply toothed or serrated, together with clumps of low shrubs, as kalmia, Andromeda, annona pygmea, myrica cerifera, empertrum, vaccinium, and others.

We now ascend a little again, and pass through a narrow pine forest; when suddenly opens to view a vastly extensive and sedgy marsh, expanding southerly like an open fan, seemingly as boundless as the great ocean: our road crossing the head of it, about three hundred yards over; the bottom here was hard sand, a foot or more under a soft muddy surface. The traders informed me, that these vast marshes lie on the borders of a great lake, many miles in length, in magnitude exceeding Lake George, and communicating with St. Juan's by a river; its confluence above the lower store at the Little Lake.

Observed as we passed over the same hills, the dens of the great land tortoise, called gopher: this strange creature remains yet undescribed by historians and travellers. The first signs of this animal's existence, as we travel southerly, are immediately after we cross the Savanna River. It is to be seen only on the high dry sand hills. When arrived at its greatest magnitude, the upper shell is near eighteen inches in length, and ten or twelve inches in breadth; the back is very high, and the shell of a very hard bony substance, consisting of many regular compartments, united by sutures, in the manner of the other species of tortoise, and covered with thin horny plates. The nether or belly shell is large, and regularly divided transversely into five parts:

these compartments are not knit together like the sutures of the skull, or the back shell of the tortoise, but adhere, or are connected together by a very ridgy horny cartilage, which serves as hinges for him to shut up his body within his shell at pleasure. The fore part of the belly shell towards its extremity is formed somewhat like a spade, extends forward near three inches, and is about an inch and an half in breadth; its extremity is a little bifid; the posterior division of the belly shell is likewise pretended backwards considerably, and is deeply bifurcated.

The legs and feet are covered with flat horny squamae; he seems to have no clefts in them or toes, but long flattish nails or talons, somewhat in resemblance to the nails of the human fingers, five on the fore feet; the hind legs or feet appear as if truncated, or as stumps of feet, armed all round with sharp, flattish strong nails, the number undetermined or irregular; the head is of a moderate size; the upper mandible a little hooked, the edges hard and sharp; the eyes are large; the nose picked; the nostrils near together and very minute; the general color of the animal is a light ash or clay, and at a distance, unless it is in motion, any one would disregard or overlook it as a stone or an old stump. It is astonishing what a weight one of these creatures will bear; it will easily carry any man standing on its back, on level ground. They form great and deep dens in the sand hills, casting out incredible quantities of earth. They are esteemed excellent food. The eggs are larger than a musket ball, perfectly round, and the shell hard.

THE TORTOISE AND
HIS FROG WIFE
Algerian folktale

The froggy went a'courting, to the tortoise's chagrin.

Have you ever heard the story about the frog who married the tortoise?

Well, she did, and she was well-behaved. But one day she cried out, "Tortoise, I want meat!" "You have only to ask me, my beloved," said the tortoise. "Let us go down to the wadi to the cattle's water hole. I'll kill a cow for you to eat." And they went to the wadi, the tortoise slowly walking ahead, and his frog wife hopping along behind.

They came to the wadi, where the cattle were drinking water after a rainfall. The tortoise waddled up to a cow and sank its beak into the cow's hind leg. The cow kicked hard, and the tortoise went flying high into the air, landing on his back. The tortoise waved its legs in the air, helpless and angry.

The frog wife stood over him and chided him for his fecklessness, and then she hopped off to her hole.

After a while the rain fell again, and the water in the wadi rose and lifted the tortoise so that he could get back on his feet. He waddled home to his wife.

"Who's there?" cried the frog when she heard the tortoise coming up the path.

"It's me, your loving husband," the tortoise answered.

"I have no husband!" the frog yelled. "I have divorced him because he cannot provide for me!"

Heartbroken, the tortoise turned and went out into the road, hoping that a cart would come along and put him out of his misery. A cart did come by, but the donkey guiding it stopped and said, "Why are you so sad, uncle?"

"Oh," cried the tortoise, "my wife has left me. Can you make her come back to me?"

The donkey went up and knocked on the frog's door.

"Who is it?" called the frog. "I am not expecting guests!"

"It's me, donkey," he said. "I beg you in the name of Allah the Merciful to show kindness to your husband and take him back."

"Go away, you braying ass, you scavenger, you dust-coated donkey!" cried the frog.

The donkey stomped away, leaving the tortoise to bewail the loss of his wife.

Then a horse came along and saw the tortoise. "What's the matter?" he asked.

"My wife is gone," said the tortoise. "You are so well-bred, perhaps she'll listen to you. Can you ask her to take me back?"

The horse knocked at the frog's door.

"Who is it?" the frog demanded. "I am not expecting guests!"

"It's me, the horse. I beg you in the name of the Maker to go back to your husband's tent!"

"Go away, you long-faced, whinnying, hobbledy horse!" cried the frog.

The horse stomped away, while the tortoise stood in the road weeping.

Then a hen saw the tortoise and asked, "What's wrong? Why are you so sad?"

"My true love is gone," said the tortoise. "Could you talk to her, woman to woman, and ask her to come back to me?"

The hen knocked at the frog's door.

"Who is it?" the frog asked. "I live here alone. Leave me be!"

"It's me, the hen. I ask you in the name of the Creator to come with me back to your husband's tent!"

"Go away, you slum-dwelling, foul-smelling, egg-laying wretch!" said the frog.

The hen left, cackling, while the tortoise kept on weeping.

At last a serpent slithered along and said to tortoise, "What has happened here? Why are you so sad?"

"O serpent," the tortoise sniffled, "my wife has divorced me. Can you make her change her mind?"

The serpent went to the frog's door, but he did not bother to knock. He did not stand on ceremony but slid down into her damp hole without knocking. He hissed at her, "Listen, frog, you're not so dumb. Go to your tortoise husband before I puncture your hard heart with my fangs!"

The frog did just as the serpent demanded, first daubing kohl on her eyes and putting on a pair of gold earrings. Then she went with the serpent to the tortoise.

When she arrived, the tortoise said, "There you are, you evil-tempered, popeyed, splotchy, no-eared...."

But the frog interrupted him, saying, "It is the gold in my ears that makes them seem small, and the beauty of my silk gown that makes my skin seem splotchy, and the kohl on my eyes that make them seem buggy. But what about you, you stingy, slow, crusty…."

But the turtle interrupted her, saying, "My coat is as fine as the best Tunisian cloth, my boots of the finest Spanish leather."

The tortoise and the frog saw that they were perfectly matched. They embraced each other, and they returned to their home.

TURTLE MAGIC
Pliny the Elder

*Of what use are turtles? The Roman naturalist Pliny the Elder
had some ideas.*

Like the beaver, the tortoise is amphibious. It shares the
same medical properties, but it costs more than the beaver
because of its unusual shape. The blood of a tortoise
improves the eyesight and removes cataracts. It is also a spe-
cific antidote for snakebite, and for the poisons of spiders
and other venomous creatures. Tortoise flesh is also good to
burn in fumigating a house against evil spirits, and for
counteracting magical spells and potions that witches have
cast. Tortoises are really not very common here in Italy, but
they are in Africa.

translated by Gregory McNamee

LOGGERHEADS

Thomas Barbour

Director of the Museum of Comparative Zoology at Harvard University, Thomas Barbour (1885–1946) traveled the world to seek rare specimens for his collections. A hunter of a kind himself, he was still troubled by the trade in turtles that prevailed in the Caribbean in his day—a trade that, thanks to the work of international conservation groups, has since lessened.

It was in the Bahamas on another occasion that I saw an interesting sight. A giant loggerhead turtle, floating lazily on the surface, would swim up to and gulp down Portuguese men-of-war, or Physalias, which were floating about abundantly. The old turtle would ease up to the Physalia, close his eyes, and make a snap for it. I suspect that the hard, horny jaws and the tough skin were impervious to the painful stinging caused by the nettle cells of the Siphonophore's tentacles, but that probably the tender skin about its eyes offered no such protection and the blind gulps were to protect these areas.

The loggerhead, not being fit to eat, is still an abundant sea turtle all through the West Indian area. Green turtles have grown scarce because they have been hunted so constantly. They are brought to Limon in Costa Rica for shipment to the aldermen's feasts in London, being carried in individual tanks on the forward deck of the fruit liners crossing the ocean. Kindhearted persons often are hurt by seeing the turtles kept lying on their backs. They little realize that if they were kept lying plastron down, which would be their natural position, they would soon die, the lower shell being weakly constructed and incapable of long supporting the weight of the turtles. I am sure this would not apply to small individuals, but I have been informed by many turtlers that it is dangerous to leave big, heavy turtles on their stomachs for very long.

Once, climbing up a high cliff overlooking clear, still water along the shore of New Providence Island, I frightened two turtles which had been grazing on seaweeds on the bottom quite close to shore. One was a green turtle and one a so-called Ridley, another species altogether. Both turtles raced away, the green turtle quite deliberately and the Ridley with an astounding burst of speed. My friend Dr. Archie F. Carr, Jr., of the University of Florida, who is an authority on turtles, has noticed this same fact on a number of occasions, and he tells me that, unlike all other sea turtles, the Ridley when brought ashore snaps about in such a blind rage that it tires itself out and would probably fidget and worry itself to death in a short time if allowed to do so. Sea turtles are fascinating critters and it is a pity that the demand for tortoise shell has brought one magnificent animal as close to extinction as the delicacy of its flesh has brought another.

Georgetown, Grand Cayman, which we visited on several occasions, is the center of the green-turtle industry. The Cayman Islanders are expert boatbuilders, and their fast-sailing schooners comb the cays of British Honduras and Nicaragua, turtling for soup meat. I have been told that most of the turtles are caught with a bullen, an iron hoop to which is attached a deep net. The schooner anchors. The small boats set out with one man to scull in the stern and another in the bow peering down into the clear water with a bucket having a glass bottom, called a water glass. When a green turtle is spied resting on the bottom the bullen is let down as close to it as possible, a rope being attached to the apex of the net. The instant the iron ring strikes bottom the turtle gives a surprised leap upward, pushes its four fins out through the coarse mesh of the net and, thus entangled, may be drawn to the surface. Turtles, of course, are also "pegged" with a harpoon having a little head which comes loose, with a line attached. But this is less satisfactory in that turtles may be badly injured, hence less likely to survive the long sea voyage to market.

They seem pitiful objects, with their great fins folded across their breasts made fast with a bit of binder twine rove through holes cut in their flippers. But I suspect that this really doesn't hurt the turtle very much, as they seem to pay little attention to much more shocking injuries. Individuals are often seen that have lost a large part of one or more flippers, so that in some cases they can swim only with difficulty. This is commonly supposed to be the work of sharks. But I think it is much more likely that the injuries are caused by fighting with other turtles. There is always great excitement when the turtle schooners come to Key West. One Cayman vessel will often carry a hundred or more turtles stacked in its hold. They probably average 200 pounds apiece and the cargo is a very valuable one.

THE SEDITIOUS TORTOISE
Igbo folktale

In this African story, tortoise dons revolutionary garb.

Tiger once hired all the animals in the forest to work on his farm. He did not hire Tortoise, and Tortoise was angry. He asked around, and he was told that Tiger had not hired him because, so Tiger thought, he was too weak to do the hard work of farming.

Tortoise was enraged, and he plotted vengeance. When the animals were waiting for their noontime meal at Tiger's farm, he burrowed beneath them and, plucking his lyre, began to sing a song:

Stupid animals working for Tiger
Stop your hoeing and planting
Why break your backs for another man's wealth?
Save your labors for your own rewards
Stupid animals working for Tiger

The animals who heard this song became discontented, especially because the food had not arrived from Tiger's kitchen. The ass said, "Tiger doesn't seem to care that we can work only when our stomachs are full." The crane agreed, and so did the elephant. And eventually the animals began to drift away from the farm, while Tortoise played even more energetically, sowing rebellion.

Then Tortoise appeared and said to Tiger, "You thought I was weak, but look at how strong I truly am. Just by playing a few bars of a song I can bend these animals to do my will. Remember that, O Tiger, the next time you make assumptions about who can and cannot work."

TURTLE SOUP

Lewis Carroll

To appreciate a turtle, thank goodness, is not necessarily to appreciate turtle soup. Nonetheless, that is what Lewis Carroll does in Alice's Adventures in Wonderland, *a book full of ironic moments.*

Beautiful soup, so rich and green,
Waiting for a hot tureen!
Who for such dainties would not stoop?
Soup of the evening, beautiful soup!

Beautiful soup! Who cares for fish,
Game, or any other dish?
Who would not give all else for two
Pennyworth only of beautiful soup?

THE CHILDREN AND
THE TORTOISE
Gunwinggu folktale

The Gunwinggu, an aboriginal people of northern Australia, tell this story, the point of which seems to be that while people may hunt for turtles, turtles are not supposed to hunt for people.

At the headwaters of the Liverpool River, a group of children went down to swim. They made a circle around a boy in the middle, and then they splashed the water with their hands. The boy dived down under them, swam under the ring, and came up behind them where they could not see him. The other children looked for him until one of them saw him. Then they cried, "There he is!" They saw him, but he swam fast, and they couldn't tag that boy.

Ngalmangiyi, Long-necked Tortoise Woman, was also in the water. She pretended to help the children catch the boy, and she stole him away. The boy escaped, though.

Ganawaiwai, Diving Duck Woman, saw where the boy was and cried out to the children, "There he is! We must catch that boy!"

"What about you, Tortoise?" they asked. "Can you catch him?" "I'm not very good at catching him," she replied. "What about you, Duck?" they asked. "Can you catch him?" "I'll try," Diving Duck Woman answered. As the boy fled from Diving Duck Woman, Tortoise got hold of him and dragged him under the water, singing, *gabun-garagara bir bir yul,* "Swimming along, making tracks on the river-bank."

Long-necked Tortoise Woman's children were waiting for her under the water. They saw the boy that their mother had brought for them. "What do you have there?" they asked. "Food," she said. "But it might not be good."

They skewered the boy with a spear and ate him. But he was no good, and they all vomited. Later, when their lives were over, they all turned into rocks there at the headwaters of the Liverpool River, where you can see them today.

THE HUNGRY SPIDER
AND THE TURTLE
Ashante folktale

The Ashante of West Africa tell this story about a disastrous episode in the annals of animal etiquette.

Spider was hungry. But then Spider was always hungry, so much so that everyone took pains to avoid him lest they meet him on the street and, as the rules of hospitality demand, have to invite him home for dinner.

One day a turtle came into town from the backcountry. This turtle was hot and tired, and the first person he happened to meet was Spider, who had to invite him for supper, as the rules of hospitality demand. Spider was not eager to share his provisions, you see, but he was even less eager to have people say of him that he was miserly.

The turtle sat down to eat. But Spider said, "Wait. Go wash up before you eat. There's a little spring behind the house."

The turtle waddled down the trail to the spring and washed his face. Then he waddled back to Spider's house, getting dust all over himself so that his face was soon just as dirty as it was before he washed himself.

Spider said, "Your feet are dirty. Please go and wash them off before we eat." By that time the food was on the table, and the turtle was nearly faint with hunger. Still, he turned, waddled off, and washed himself. Just as quickly, the dust made him dirty before he could take his place at Spider's table, and Spider kept sending him back to clean up.

By the time the turtle returned to the table, Spider had eaten everything. "Thank you for being my guest," Spider said. "Wasn't that a fine meal we enjoyed?"

The turtle thanked Spider for his hospitality, and he lumbered away. Although he could have complained about Spider's behavior, he did not.

Not long after that, Spider found himself far from home. He called on the turtle to ask for something to eat.

"Wait here," said the turtle. "I'll just go down to the bottom of the river and find something for us to eat."

The turtle disappeared under the surface of the water for a long time. Spider was famished. He paced back and forth, waiting for the turtle to return. Finally, impatient, he jumped into the water, but he was too light to make his way under the current to find the turtle.

In time the turtle bobbed up and said, "What's the matter? Aren't you hungry?"

Spider said, "Yes, I'm starved."

"Well, then," the turtle said. "Come down to my house and we'll eat!"

The turtle then dived down to the bottom of the river.

Spider floated on the surface for a while. Then he picked up a pebble with his jaws and sank to the bottom. When he arrived, the turtle was just finishing up his meal. "Wasn't that a delicious dinner we enjoyed?" he asked Spider. "It was almost as good as the one you served me the other day."

That is why you seldom see spiders and turtles dining together.

CAYOU CAOUAN: SOJOURN OF A SNAPPER
Rocklin G.

A Cajun storyteller relates a curious bit of Louisiana folklore, in which turtles and a rare bayou Bigfoot sighting combine to show us that folktales are ever-evolving, adapting new elements as they develop.

I can still remember when I firs' come out my shell, me.

My mama lef' word abo't what to do when I come out. She said I had to be careful of anyt'ing bigger dan me. *Mai sha* [but yes], when I look out that crack in my eggshell, everyt'ing was bigger than me. As fo' me, I was no bigger than a cayou—that's a li'l tiny rock.

She said fo' me to head fo' the water, then to dig a hole in the mud and jus' wait wit' my mout' open and eat whatever come by. That's what I did, me. And sho' enough, all kind li'l fish and bug come aroun' fo' me to eat. The only other t'ing she warn me abo't was the two-legged monsters that come to trap us, then skin us alive and eat us up. A long time pass by, and I almost fo'got abo't all that, wit' all the food there was to eat. I can't believe, me, I start out a cayou and now weigh fifty pound with my eggs.

I got big and fat and didn't have to go nowhere, no. Then one day a big ol' hairy two-legged put his foot in my mout' and I close my mout' shut. *Coo tee chien!* I heard the loudest noise coming from o't the water, and then my mout' start shaking like you can't believe. I got so dizzy, I let go of that Boggy Creek bigfoot. It was too big fo' me to swallow anyway.

I start to swim away, when that big muddy t'ing pick me up and flung me over the water.

When I splash down, I was still spinning and then I went over the spillway into the bayou. And that two-legged monster was right behind me, him, 'cause I heard him splash after me. I was lucky, me, 'cause the current pull me real fast down the bayou.

That's okay, *sha*. I got a good look at that ugly t'ing with long hair all over his body. And that smell, *sha tee bebe*, would even turn a turtle away. From now on, I'm gonna be on the looko't, yeah!

I was caught in that current fo' a long time, and I didn't know where it was take me. I felt like I had swallow up half the bayou by the time I caught myse'f on a log.

Boy, I was glad fo' that, me. I climb on that log so I could dry myse'f in the sun.

I was floatin' on that log lookin' fo' a new place to live. I musta gone twenty mile down the bayou, when I come across some strange lookin' critters hangin' on a big ol' tree layin' across the bayou. On the ot'er side of them, I saw the front part of a boat stickin' o't the bayou and goin' roun' and roun'. Then one of them strange creature let go and disappear under the water.

They's three more and they start screamin', like they was never gonna see him again. *Mais sha*, I roll off that log and dive in to see if I can fin' him. The current got stronger and stronger and I start to go roun' and roun' like that boat. *Tonnerre m'ecrase* [lit., thunder erase me] I was caught up in that whirlpool, me too, yeah!

Mais sha, when I bump into that critter, I found o't he had two leg. *Crotte de gam* [lit., rooster shit], I had some vision right there of turtle sauce picante wit' me in the middle. That's what they liable to do wit' us, give 'em half the chance.

It was too late fo' me then my friend, fo' that two-legged done hook onto my spike on my back. I want to snap at him, but I just couldn' reach far enough. I swam till I couldn' swin no mo'.

We landed on the muddy bank. Lucky fo' me, he let me go. And I was gonna leave, too, but I smelled some meat. *Mais sha,* I was too hongry to go anywhere.

Them two-legged critter didn't try to catch me, no. Instead, they t'rew me a big piece of pig tasso [bacon]. It smell like it was burn up and when I ate it, it was so good, it make you want to slap yo' mama. Anyway, them ot'er two-legged creatures were sure glad to see their friend still alive. They even t'rew me anoter piece and me, I snap it up.

Then they climb back on that tree and climb back up on the bank of Cocodrie. *Mais sha,* I was still hongry, me. So me too, I climb up on the bank of Cocodrie, and I dig a hole to reach the top. Abo't the time I make it to the top, I got a whiff of that two-legged boggy-beast from befo'. *Mais sha tee neg!* I was afraid fo' them boatmen. That's when I knew I'd have to hurry and catch up wit'them so I could he'p them if that big muddy t'ing come aroun' again. And that was no easy job fo' somebody slow like me, no!

It was way pass dark befo' I got to the top of the bayou bank, then I smell their tracks and follow them tracks till abo't midnight. They still had a fire going, but the weather had turned to the north—a big storm was comin', yeah.

Them Cajun creature was abo't as lucky as you can get, 'cause they had save their food, their sleepin' sacks, and the boat and motor, even if it didn't start up. But that wasn't gone he'p protec' them from that big storm, no. They had made camp close to a li'l caban where the owner feed the calf runnin' aroun'. When the col' wind and the rain came, they got under that caban and block the rain wit' a sleepin' sack. They was sure quiet fo' the rest o' the night after that storm come crashin' by.

Me, I foun' a muddy hole and I dug me a place to sleep. Lucky fo' me, my tongue got a built-in worm bait. I ate all the crawfish that pass by my mout'. Them crazy crawfish t'ought my tongue was somet'ing to eat, but I eat them. When they foun' out what it is, it was too late—I done swallow them whole, head and all.

The nex' mornin' the sky was clear, and the win' had died down to a li'l breeze comin' from the woods over there. Them Cajun critter got up real early to get ready fo' the las' stretch of the bayou. They woke me up when I hear them rippin' the cypress board off the caban nex' to the mud hole where I was sleepin', me. I kinda stick my head out the water and sho enough, they got a fire going and they was burnin' boudin on some long sticks. Then they tore off another board, *pouyie*, I pass some gas real loud and come flyin' o't the water. It musta been them crawfish give me that gas, yeah.

Mais sha, they laugh to see me jump like that. They was glad to see me too, 'cause they threw me some boudin, all I could eat. Mmmm, that some smelly stuff. I woulda like it better, me, if it had been a li'l mo' rotten. You know what I mean, hon. The kind of stink that don't wash off fo' nothin'.

After I was done eatin' and they was abo't done makin' their paddles, I was smellin' fo' some more boudin, me, when I got a stinch of that skinny two-legged ogre that almos' caught my ass the day before. I start splashin' in the water wit' my feet to let them know abo't the mad two-legged boggy brute. And instead of takin' notice of that damn t'ing, they t'row me another piece of boudin. And me, I stretch my neck real long and snatch that dead pig meat. After that, *coooo ... tee neg,* them four two-legged Cajun was scramblin' to do the alligator two-step. *Mais sha,* it happen so fast, I don't know what happen to them. That big two-legged boggy critter come runnin' into camp. I saw them pick up the paddle and run fo' the bayou.

That hairy bigfoot come runnin' toward my face and I jus' open my mout' and snap it closed. There come that same holler again, except a lot louder this time. I took hold of him good and this time I wasn't lettin' go. He kept tryin' to kick me off, till all of a sudden I was flyin' in the air again with two big toes in my mout'. I didn't stop till I landed on that li'l caban.

That mean-lookin' t'ing took the last of my boudin, but that's okay, *sha*. Me, I got two juicy toes. I want you to know that bigfoot holler fo' two days in the wood over there. As fo' the res' of them two-leggeds, they was still runnin' toward the bayou. When they got to the cliff along the shore, they jump, one by one, in that hole I dug and they disappear fo' good. They ain't never come back.

THE WONDERFUL TURTLE
Chippewa folktale

Do you know why poor cuckolded Turtle has a flat stomach? The Chippewa do, as this folktale relates.

Near a Chippewa village lay a large lake, and in this lake there lived an enormous turtle. This was no ordinary turtle, as he would often come out of his home in the lake and visit with his Indian neighbors. He paid the most of his visits to the head chief, and on these occasions would stay for hours, smoking and talking with him.

The chief, seeing that the turtle was very smart and showed great wisdom in his talk, took a great fancy to him, and whenever any puzzling subject came up before the chief, he generally sent for Turtle to help him decide.

One day there came a great misunderstanding between different parties of the tribe, and so excited became both sides that it threatened to cause bloodshed. The chief was unable to decide for either faction, so he said, "I will call Turtle. He will judge for you."

Sending for the turtle, the chief vacated his seat for the time being, until the turtle should hear both sides, and decide which was in the right. The turtle came, and taking the chief's seat, listened very attentively to both sides, and thought long before he gave his decision. After thinking long and studying each side carefully, he came to the conclusion to decide in favor of both. This would not cause any hard feelings. So he gave them a lengthy speech and showed them where they were both in the right, saying: "You are both in the right in some ways and wrong in others. Therefore, I will say that you both are equally in the right."

When they heard this decision, they saw that the turtle was right, and gave him a long cheer for the wisdom he displayed. The whole tribe saw that had it not been for this wise decision there would have been a great shedding of blood in the tribe. So they voted him as their judge, and the chief, being so well pleased with him, gave to him his only daughter in marriage.

The daughter of the chief was the most beautiful maiden of the Chippewa nation, and young men from other tribes traveled hundreds of miles for an opportunity to make love to her, and try to win her for a wife. It was all to no purpose. She would accept no one, only him whom her father would select for her. The turtle was very homely, but as he was prudent and wise, the father chose him, and she accepted him.

The young men of the tribe were very jealous, but their jealousy was all to no purpose. She married the turtle. The young men would make sport of the chief's son-in-law. They would say to him: "How did you come to have so flat a stomach?" The turtle answered them, saying: "My friends, had you been in my place, you too would have flat stomachs. I came by my flat stomach in this way: The Chippewas and Sioux had a great battle, and the Sioux, too numerous for the Chippewas, were killing them off so fast that they had to run for their lives. I was on the Chippewa side and some of the Sioux were pressing five of us, and were gaining on us very fast. Coming to some high grass, I threw myself down flat on my face, and pressed my stomach close to the ground, so the pursuers could not see me. They passed me and killed the four I was with. After they had gone back, I arose and lo! my stomach was as you see it now. So hard had I pressed to the ground that it would not assume its original shape again."

After he had explained the cause of his deformity to them, they said: "The Turtle is brave. We will bother him no more."

Shortly after this the Sioux attacked the Chippewas, and everyone deserted the village. The turtle could not travel as fast as the rest and was left behind. It being an unusually hot day in the fall, the turtle grew very thirsty and sleepy. Finally, scenting water, he crawled toward the point from whence the scent came, and coming to a large lake jumped in and had a bath, after which he swam toward the center and dived down, and finding some fine large rocks at the bottom, he crawled in among them and fell asleep. He had his sleep out and rose to the top.

Swimming to shore he found it was summer. He had slept all winter. The birds were singing, and the green grass and leaves gave forth a sweet odor.

He crawled out and started out looking for the Chippewa camp. He came upon the camp several days after he had left his winter quarters, and going around in search of his wife, found her at the extreme edge of the village. She was nursing her baby, and as he asked to see it, she showed it to him. When he saw that it was a lovely baby and did not resemble him in any respect, he got angry and went off to a large lake, where he contented himself with catching flies and insects and living on weeds the remainder of his life.

THE COURAGE OF TURTLES

Edward Hoagland

Edward Hoagland offers a lovely celebration of chelonian familiars in his essay "The Courage of Turtles," a masterpiece of nature study done close to home.

Turtles are a kind of bird with the governor turned low. With the same attitude of removal, they cock a glance at what is going on, as if they need only to fly away. Until recently they were also a case of virtue rewarded, at least in the town where I grew up, because, being humble creatures, there were plenty of them. Even when we still had a few bobcats in the woods the local snapping turtles, growing up to forty pounds, were the largest carnivores. You would see them through the amber water, as big as greeny wash basins at the bottom of the pond, until they faded into the inscrutable mud as if they hadn't existed at all.

When I was ten I went to Dr. Green's Pond, a two-acre pond across the road. When I was twelve I walked a mile or so to Taggart's Pond, which was lusher, had big water snakes and a waterfall; and shortly after that I was bicycling way up to the adventuresome vastness of Mud Pond, a lake-sized body of water in the reservoir system of a Connecticut city, possessed of cat-backed little islands and empty shacks and a forest of pines and hardwoods along the shore. Otters, foxes and mink left their prints on the bank; there were pike and perch. As I got older, the estates and forgotten back lots in town were parceled out and sold for nice prices, yet, though the woods had shrunk, it seemed that fewer people walked in the woods. The new residents didn't know how to find them. Eventually, exploring, they did find them, and it required some ingenuity and doubling around on my part to go for eight miles without meeting someone. I was grown by now, I lived in New York, and that's what I wanted on the occasional weekends when I came out.

Since Mud Pond contained drinking water I had felt confident nothing untoward would happen there. For a long while the developers stayed away, until the drought of the mid-1960s. This event, squeezing the edges in, convinced the local water company that the pond really wasn't a necessity as a catch basin, however; so they bulldozed a hole in the earthen dam, bulldozed the banks to fill in the bottom, and landscaped the flow of water that remained to wind like an English brook and provide a domestic view for the houses which were planned. Most of the painted turtles of Mud Pond, who had been inaccessible as they sunned on their rocks, wound up in boxes in boys' closets within a matter of days. Their footsteps in the dry leaves gave them away as they wandered forlornly. The snappers and the little musk turtles, neither of whom leave the water except once a year to lay their eggs, dug into the drying mud for another siege of hot weather, which they were accustomed to doing whenever the pond got low. But this time it was low for good; the mud baked over them and slowly entombed them. As for the ducks, I couldn't stroll in the woods and not feel guilty, because they were crouched beside every stagnant pothole, or were slinking between the bushes with their heads tucked into their shoulders so that I wouldn't see them. If they decided I had, they beat their way up through the screen of trees, striking their wings dangerously, and wheeled about with that headlong, magnificent velocity to locate another poor puddle.

I used to catch possums and black snakes as well as turtles, and I kept dogs and goats. Some summers I worked in a menagerie with the big personalities of the animal kingdom, like elephants and rhinoceroses. I was twenty before these enthusiasms began to wane, and it was then that I picked turtles as the particular animal I wanted to keep in touch with. I was allergic to fur, for one thing, and turtles need minimal care and not much in the way of quarters. They're personable beasts. They see the same colors we do and they seem to see just as well, as one discovers in trying to sneak up on them. In the laboratory they unravel the twists of a maze with the hot-blooded rapidity of a mammal. Though they can't run as fast as a rat, they improve on their errors just as quickly, pausing at each crossroads to look left and right. And they rock rhythmically in place, as we often do, although they are hatched from eggs, not the womb. (A common explanation psychologists give for our pleasure in rocking quietly is that it recapitulates our mother's heartbeat *in utero*.)

Snakes, by contrast, are dryly silent and priapic. They are smooth movers, legalistic, unblinking, and they afford the humor which the humorless do. But they make challenging captives; sometimes they don't eat for months on a point of order—if the light isn't right, for instance. Alligators are sticklers too. They're like war-horses, or German shepherds, and with their bar-shaped, vertical pupils adding emphasis, they have the *idée fixe* of eating, eating, even when they choose to refuse all food and stubbornly die. They delight in tossing a salamander up towards the sky and grabbing him in their long mouths as he comes down. They're so eager that they get the jitters, and they're too much of a proposition for a casual aquarium like mine. Frogs are depressingly defenseless: that moist, extensive back, with the bones almost sticking through. Hold a frog and you're holding its skeleton. Frogs tasty legs are the staff of life to many animals— herons, raccoons, ribbon snakes—though they themselves are hard to feed. It's not an enviable role to be the staff of life, and after frogs you descend down the evolutionary ladder a big step to fish.

Turtles cough, burp, whistle, grunt and hiss, and produce social judgments. They put their heads together amicably enough, but then one drives the other back with the suddenness of two dogs who have been conversing in tones too low for an onlooker to hear. They pee in fear when they're first caught, but exercise both pluck and optimism in trying to escape, walking for hundreds of yards within the confines of their pen, carrying the weight of that cumbersome box on legs which are cruelly positioned for walking. They don't feel that the contest is unfair; they keep plugging, rolling like sailorly souls—a bobbing, infirm gait, a brave, sea-legged momentum—stopping occasionally to study the lay of the land. For me, anyway, they manage to contain the rest of the animal world. They can stretch out their necks like a giraffe, or loom underwater like an apocryphal hippo. They browse on lettuce thrown on the water like a cow moose which is partly submerged. They have a penguin's alertness, combined with a build like a Brontosaurus when they rise up on tiptoe. Then they hunch and ponderously lunge like a grizzly going forward.

Baby turtles in a turtle bowl are a puzzle in geometries. They're as decorative as pansy petals, but they are also self-directed building blocks, propping themselves on one another in different arrangements, before upending the tower. The timid individuals turn fearless, or vice versa. If one gets a bit arrogant he will push the others off the rock and afterwards climb down into the water and cling to the back of one of those he has bullied, tickling him with his hind feet until he bucks like a bronco. On the other hand, when this same milder-mannered fellow isn't exerting himself, he will stare right into the face of the sun for hours. What could be more lionlike? And he's at home in or out of the water and does lots of metaphysical tilting. He sinks and rises, with an infinity of levels to choose from; or, elongating himself, he climbs out on the land again to perambulate, sits boxed in his box, and finally slides back in the water, submerging into dreams.

I have five of these babies in a kidney-shaped bowl. The hatchling, who is a painted turtle, is not as large as the top joint of my thumb. He eats chicken gladly. Other foods he will attempt to eat but not with sufficient perseverance to succeed because he's so little. The yellow-bellied terrapin is probably a yearling, and he eats salad voraciously, but no meat, fish or fowl. The Cumberland terrapin won't touch salad or chicken but eats fish and all of the meats except for bacon. The little snapper, with a black crenelated shell, feasts on any kind of meat, but rejects greens and fish. The fifth of the turtles is African. I acquired him only recently and don't know him well. A mottled brown, he unnerves the green turtles, dragging their food off to his lairs. He doesn't seem to want to be green—he bites the algae off his shell, hanging meanwhile at daring, steep, head-first angles.

The snapper was a Ferdinand until I provided him with deeper water. Now he snaps at my pencil with his down-turned and fearsome mouth, his swollen face like a napalm victim's. The Cumberland has an elliptical red mark on the side of his green-and-yellow head. He is benign by nature and ought to be as elegant as his scientific name (*Pseudemys scripts elegans*), except he has contracted a disease of the air bladder which has permanently inflated it; he floats high in the water at an undignified slant and can't go under. There may have been internal bleeding, too, because his carapace is stained along its ridge. Unfortunately, like flowers, baby turtles often die. Their mouths fill up with a white fungus and their lungs with pneumonia. Their organs clog up from the rust in the water, or diet troubles, and, like a dying man's, their eyes and heads become too prominent. Toward the end, the edge of the shell becomes flabby as felt and folds around them like a shroud.

While they live they're like puppies. Although they're vivacious, they would be a bore to be with all the time, so I also have an adult wood turtle about six inches long. Her shell is the equal of any seashell for sculpturing, even a Cellini shell; it's like an old, dusty, richly engraved medallion dug out of a hillside. Her legs are salmon-orange bordered with black and protected by canted, heroic scales. Her plastron—the bottom shell—is splotched like a margay cat's coat, with black ocelli on a yellow background. It is convex to make room for the female organs inside, whereas a male's would be concave to help him fit tightly on top of her. Altogether, she exhibits every camouflage color on her limbs and shells. She has a turtleneck neck, a tail like an elephant's, wise old pachydermous hind legs and the face of a turkey—except that when I carry her she gazes at the passing ground with a hawk's eyes and mouth. Her feet fit to the fingers of my hand, one to each one, and she rides looking down. She can walk on the floor in perfect silence, but usually she lets her shell knock portentously, like a footstep, so that she resembles some grand, concise, slow-moving id. But if an earthworm is presented, she jerks swiftly ahead, poises above it and strikes like a mongoose, consuming it with wild vigor. Yet she will climb on my lap to eat bread or boiled eggs.

If put into a creek, she swims like a cutter, nosing forward to intercept a strange turtle and smell him. She drifts with the current to go downstream, maneuvering behind a rock when she wants to take stock, or sinking to the nether levels, while bubbles float up. Getting out, choosing her path, she will proceed a distance and dig into a pile of humus, thrusting herself to the coolest layer at the bottom. The hole closes over her until it's as small as a mouse's hole. She's not as aquatic as a musk turtle, not quite as terrestrial as the box turtles in the same woods, but because of her versatility she's marvelous, she's everywhere. And though she breathes the way we breathe, with scarcely perceptible movements of her chest, sometimes instead she pumps her throat ruminatively, like a pipe smoker sucking and puffing. She waits and blinks, pumping her throat, turning her head, then sets off like a loping tiger in slow motion, hurdling the jungly lumber, the pea vine and twigs. She estimates angles so well that when she rides over the rocks, sliding down a drop-off with her rugged front legs extended, she has the grace of a rodeo mare.

But she's well off to be with me rather than at Mud Pond. The other turtles have fled—those that aren't baked into the bottom. Creeping up the brooks to sad, constricted marshes, burdened as they are with that box on their backs, they're walking into a setup where all their enemies move thirty times faster than they. It's like the nightmare most of us have whimpered through, where we are weighted down disastrously while trying to flee; fleeing our home ground, we try to run.

I've seen turtles in still worse straits. On Broadway, in New York, there is a penny arcade which used to sell baby terrapins that were scrawled with bon mots in enamel paint, such as KISS ME BABY. The manager turned out to be a wholesaler as well, and once I asked him whether he had any larger turtles to sell. He took me upstairs to a loft room devoted to the turtle business. There were desks for the paper work and a series of racks that held shallow tin bins atop one another, each with several hundred babies crawling around in it. He was a smudgy-complexioned, serious fellow and he did have a few adult terrapins, but I was going to school and wasn't actually planning to buy; I'd only wanted to see them. They were aquatic turtles, but here they went without water, presumably for weeks, lurching about in those dry bins like handicapped citizens, living on gumption. An easel where the artist worked stood in the middle of the floor. She had a palette and a clip attachment for fastening the babies in place. She wore a smock and a beret, and was homely, short and eccentric-looking, with funny black hair, like some of the ladies who show their paintings in Washington Square in May. She had a cold, she was smoking, and her hand wasn't very steady, although she worked quickly enough. The smile that she produced for me would have looked giddy if she had been happier, or drunk. Of course the turtles' doom was sealed when she painted them, because their bodies inside would continue to grow but their shells would not. Gradually, invisibly, they would be crushed. Around us their bellies—two thousand belly shells—rubbed on the bins with a mournful, momentous hiss.

Somehow there were so many of them I didn't rescue one. Years later, however, I was walking on First Avenue when I noticed a basket of living turtles in front of a fish store. They were as dry as a heap of old bones in the sun;

nevertheless, they were creeping over one another gimpily, doing their best to escape. I looked and was touched to discover that they appeared to be wood turtles, my favorites, so I bought one. In my apartment I looked closer and realized that in fact this was a diamondback terrapin, which was bad news. Diamondbacks are tidewater turtles from brackish estuaries, and I had no sea water to keep him in. He spent his days thumping interminably against the baseboards, pushing for an opening through the wall. He drank thirstily but would not eat and had none of the hearty, accepting qualities of wood turtles. He was morose, paler in color, sleeker and more Oriental in the carved ridges and rings that formed his shell. Though I felt sorry for him, finally I found his unrelenting presence exasperating. I carried him, struggling in a paper bag, across town to the Morton Street Pier on the Hudson. It was August but gray and windy. He was very surprised when I tossed him in; for the first time in our association, I think, he was afraid. He looked afraid as he bobbed about on top of the water, looking up at me from ten feet below. Though we were both accustomed to his resistance and rigidity, seeing him still pitiful, I recognized that I must have done the wrong thing. At least the river was salty, but it was also bottomless; the waves were too rough for him, and the tide was coming in, bumping him against the pilings underneath the pier. Too late, I realized that he wouldn't be able to swim to a peaceful inlet in New Jersey, even if he could figure out which way to swim. But since, short of diving in after him, there was nothing I could do, I walked away.

ELEGY FOR THE GIANT TORTOISES

Margaret Atwood

Tortoises, the Canadian poet and writer Margaret Atwood suggests in this lovely elegy, may not be long for this world. We hope that she is wrong, and that the ancient chelonians outlast their tormentors.

Let others pray for the passenger pigeon
the dodo, the whooping crane, the eskimo:
everyone must specialize.

I will confine myself to a meditation
upon the giant tortoises
withering finally on a remote island.

I concentrate in subway stations,
in parks, I can't quite see them,
they move to the peripheries of my eyes

but on the last day they will be there;
already the event
like a wave travelling shapes vision:

on the road where I stand they will materialise,
plodding past me in a straggling line
awkward without water

their small heads pondering
from side to side, their useless armour
sadder than tanks and history,

in their closed gaze ocean and sunlight paralysed,
lumbering up the steps, under the archways
toward the square glass altars

where the brittle gods are kept,
the relics of what we have destroyed,
our holy and obsolete symbols.

POSTSCRIPT

"Old man turtle ambles along the deerpath, seeking break-
fast. A strand of wild ricegrass dangles from his pincer-like
beak. His small wise droll redrimmed eyes look from side
to side, bright and wary and shrewd."

—Edward Abbey, *Hayduke Lives!*

Scuba divers descend to the bottom of the great central
tank at Boston's Aquarium. They enter the water several
times a day to hand-feed the fish and small sharks. At the
end of each session, they drift to the floor of the tank and
await the great sea turtles. The turtles settle down before the
divers, often touching their noses to the divers' faceplates.
The divers put out their arms in a wide embrace; the turtles extend their front flippers and lay them on the humans'
shoulders. They lie like this for several minutes.

Watching this scene from the top of the tank, a staff
oceanographer is overheard saying, "Turtles are quite affec-
tionate. They're full of love."

Love. And this from a scientist. Still, a small pamphlet
describing the mating habits of the Chinese snapping turtle describes the event beginning with a "kiss."

We have always loved turtles, and we have often suspected
them of loving us. All through our history, we have certainly attributed greatly anthropomorphic values to turtles.
As this anthology should confirm. Wise, droll, bright, wary
and shrewd. But also, somehow, noble. Steadfast. Loving.

Turtles move us to admiration, even affection. But, unlike lions or alligators, they seldom seem to inspire true awe. They seem humorous to us. It might be that shell. Turtles are the original r.v.'s. Their wrinkled faces peer out of their chitinous campers like retirees tooling along the slow lane with their left blinker flashing endlessly. They're old. Edward Abbey's turtle is "145 years old—middleaged."

Perhaps it's their plodding pace. "The Tortoise and the Hare" made much of that steady gait. The tortoise was dependable and serious, while the hare was flighty in every sense. You can count on a turtle, we believe, and that has held true through Warner Brothers cartoons and hundreds of children's stories and the inexplicably flame-throwing giant Japanese snapping turtle, Gamera. Gamera might tear down Tokyo with appalling regularity, but he loves kids and sincere Japanese atomic scientists.

Hey, who could doubt Yertle the Turtle?

In *A Slender Thread*, Diane Ackerman recounts a classic turtle folktale/joke. In it, the scorpion approaches the turtle to ask for a ride across a body of water. The turtle, no fool, tells the scorpion that he is too dangerous to transport: One sting, and the turtle will sink and they'll both drown. The scorpion promises that he will not sting the turtle, and the turtle takes him on his back and begins to swim. And, of course, the scorpion stings the turtle. The turtle cries, "Why did you sting me? Now we will both drown!" And the scorpion says, "What did you expect? I am a scorpion. It is my nature to sting."

This is meant to demonstrate the nature of the scorpion. But it also speaks volumes about the turtle. Although scorpions must sting, must betray and harm us, the turtle must also behave in a certain way. And that way, as reflected in the folklore, is noble. He has to help. He has to do the right thing.

~

Although our preoccupation with turtles would seem ancient, tribal, it is fully current. The turtle is with us today. Nowhere is this reflected better than in twentieth-century literature. Even such a modern writer as Stephen King succumbs to the mythic pull of the turtle. In one of the various climaxes of his massive potboiler, *It*, King raids the American Indian mythos of the great turtle who bears the world on his back. We are confronted with a Godlike universal turtle with stars in its nails.

Part trickster, part spiritual elder, and part Gamera, King's great reptile says, "I'm the Turtle, son. I made the universe, but please don't blame me for it; I had a bellyache." What a card. King takes a moment to reassure us that the Turtle's eyes are kind. But we already knew that.

~

John Steinbeck offers us the most noble Entrance By A Turtle in the third chapter of *The Grapes of Wrath*.

Tom Joad has just been revealed to us, making his way home in the opening chapters, when Steinbeck suddenly shifts the focus to a plodding land turtle. It's a hot day, and here he comes, "turning aside for nothing, dragging his high-domed shell over the grass." The narrative camera catches him in a John Ford shot: he looms against the sky, tall from the waist up, as monumental as the desert hoodoos in a hundred John Wayne movies.

"The barley beards slid off his shell," Steinbeck writes, "and the clover burrs fell on him and rolled to the ground." The turtle is not unlike the steadfast Okies we are about to meet in the rest of the novel. Pricks and stings roll off their backs, too, as they make their long-suffering way across the unforgiving landscape.

This turtle, too, has "fierce, humorous eyes."

And on he plods, resolute and brave as he surmounts barrier after barrier. Then, just as he breaks free of the weeds and the dirt cliffs and comes out on an easier surface, we realize he's on the highway. He makes his way across all the lanes until, near the other side, approaching safety, a sedan comes speeding. The woman behind the wheel sees him, and in a fit of inexplicable meanness, aims for him and hits him, sending him skittering helplessly. Like the Okies, the force of the modern, more affluent world comes along and knocks him asunder. No fool, Steinbeck knows our sympathies lie with the turtle, not the driver—as our hopes are being directed toward the Joads and the Okies, not the "bosses."

Tom Joad finds the turtle and bundles him up and carries him away. Thus, the noble symbol of all that is admirable in the struggle actually joins the struggle. And, to make sure we get the point, Steinbeck has the next human to see Tom Joad sing, "Yes, sir, that's my Saviour...."

~

Ed Abbey's turtle is even more explicit in his symbolic role. In *Hayduke Lives!* our old friend is not only plodding along, representing all of us and apparently all of Nature, too, but he is buried alive by a monstrous Gamera-sized strip-mining machine. The monster tractor, named *Goliath* (of course), moves on, leaving the soul of the desert buried. Ed engages in some Steinbeckian nudging when he says, "Only a turtle ... could be more patient [than the despoilers of the desert]. As it waits, six feet under, for the coming of the beast."

Amen, brother.

Acknowledgments: Shauna Decker, Darrell Bourque, University of Southwest Louisiana.

Luis Alberto Urrea

BIBLIOGRAPHY

Atwood, Margaret. *Selected Poems, 1951–1975.* Boston: Houghton Mifflin, 1976.

Barbour, Thomas. *Naturalist at Large.* Boston: Atlantic Monthly, 1944.

Beckwith, Martha. *Hawaiian Mythology.* Honolulu: University of Hawaii Press, 1970.

Berger, John. *About Looking.* London: Writers and Readers, 1978.

Berndt, Ronald M., and Catherine H. Berndt. *The Speaking Land: Myth and Story in Aboriginal Australia.* Rochester, Vermont: Inner Traditions International, 1994.

Bierhorst, John. *Mythology of the Lenape.* Tucson: University of Arizona Press, 1995.

Bjorndal, Karen A., ed. *Biology and Conservation of Sea Turtles.* Washington, D.C.: Smithsonian Institution Press, 1995.

Bleek, W. H. I., and L. C. Lloyd. *Specimens of Bushman Folklore.* London: George Allen, 1911.

Burroughs, Franklin. *Billy Watson's Croker Sack.* Boston: Houghton Mifflin, 1991.

California Center for Wildlife. *Living with Wildlife.* San Francisco: Sierra Club Books, 1994.

Carroll, Lewis. *Alice's Adventures in Wonderland.* New York: Random House, 1967.

Clark, W. P. *The Indian Sign Language.* Philadelphia: L. R. Hamersly, 1885.

Courlander, Harold. *A Treasury of African Folklore.* New York: Doubleday, 1961.

Darwin, Charles. *The Voyage of the Beagle.* London: Watts, 1860.

Delphin, Gaetan. *Recueil du textes pour l'étude d l'arabe parlé.* Algiers: Éditions Maghreb, 1891.

Densmore, Frances. *Music of the Tule Indians of Panama.* Washington, D.C.: U.S. Government Printing Office, 1926.

Dobie, J. Frank, ed. *Southwestern Lore.* Austin: Texas Folklore Society, 1931.

Durham, Edith. *High Albania.* London: Edward Arnold, 1909.

Ernst, Carl H., and Roger W. Barbour. *Turtles of the World.* Washington, D.C.: Smithsonian Institution Press, 1989.

Hoagland, Edward. *The Courage of Turtles.* San Francisco: North Point Press, 1985.

Kroeber, A. L. "Indian Myths of South Central California." *American Archaeology and Ethnology* 4, 4 (1906–07): 229–31.

Liliuokalani. *Kumulipo: An Hawaiian Creation Myth.* Honolulu: Polynesian Historical Society, 1900.

Lindqvist, Cecilia. *China: Empire of Living Symbols.* Reading, Massachusetts: Addison Wesley, 1991.

Melville, Herman. *The Encantadas.* Evanston: Northwestern University Press, 1982.

Miller, Joseph. *The Arizona Story.* New York: Hastings House, 1952.

Mooney, James. *Myths of the Cherokee*. Washington, D.C.: U.S. Government Printing Office, 1900.

Pritchard, Peter. *Living Turtles of the World*. Jersey City: TFH Publications, 1967.

Quiller-Couch, Arthur, ed. *The Oxford Book of English Verse*. Oxford: Oxford University Press, 1919.

Reichel-Dolmatoff, Gerardo. *Amazonian Cosmos*. Chicago: University of Chicago Press, 1971.

Robin, P. Ansell. *Animal Lore in English Literature*. London: John Murray, 1932.

Russell, Frank. *The Pima Indians*. Washington, D.C.: U.S. Government Printing Office, 1905.

Waller, Geoffrey, ed. *Sea Life: A Complete Guide to the Marine Environment*. Washington, D.C.: Smithsonian Institution Press, 1996.

White, Gilbert. *The Natural History of Selborne*. London: John Murray, 1798.

Wintle, Justin. *The Dragon's Almanac: Chinese, Japanese, and Other Far Eastern Proverbs*. London: Routledge & Kegan Paul, 1983.